Developing Essential Understanding *of* Expressions, Equations, *and* Functions *for* Teaching Mathematics *in* Grades 6–8

Gwendolyn Lloyd
The Pennsylvania State University
University Park, Pennsylvania

Beth Herbel-Eisenmann
Michigan State University
East Lansing, Michigan

Jon R. Star
Harvard University
Cambridge, Massachusetts

Rose Mary Zbiek
Series Editor
The Pennsylvania State University
University Park, Pennsylvania

NCTM | NATIONAL COUNCIL OF TEACHERS OF MATHEMATICS

1906 Association Drive, Reston, VA 20191-1502
(703) 620-9840; (800) 235-7566; www.nctm.org

Third printing 2015

Library of Congress Cataloging-in-Publication Data

Lloyd, Gwendolyn M.
Developing essential understanding of expressions, equations, and functions for teaching mathematics in grades 6-8 / Gwendolyn Lloyd, Beth Herbel-Eisenmann, Jon R. Star.
p. cm.
Includes bibliographical references.
ISBN 978-0-87353-670-7
1. Mathematics--Study and teaching (Middle school) 2. Effective teaching. I. Herbel-Eisenmann, Beth A. II. Star, Jon R. III. Title.
QA11.2.L585 2011
513.071'2--dc23
2011034646

The National Council of Teachers of Mathematics is the public voice of mathematics education, supporting teachers to ensure equitable mathematics learning of the highest quality for all students through vision, leadership, professional development, and research.

Printed in the United States of America

Contents

Foreword

Teaching mathematics in prekindergarten–grade 12 requires a special understanding of mathematics. Effective teachers of mathematics think about and beyond the content that they teach, seeking explanations and making connections to other topics, both inside and outside mathematics. Students meet curriculum and achievement expectations when they work with teachers who know what mathematics is important for each topic that they teach.

The National Council of Teachers of Mathematics (NCTM) presents the Essential Understanding Series in tandem with a call to focus the school mathematics curriculum in the spirit of *Curriculum Focal Points for Prekindergarten through Grade 8 Mathematics: A Quest for Coherence*, published in 2006, and *Focus in High School Mathematics: Reasoning and Sense Making,* released in 2009. The Essential Understanding books are a resource for individual teachers and groups of colleagues interested in engaging in mathematical thinking to enrich and extend their own knowledge of particular mathematics topics in ways that benefit their work with students. The topic of each book is an area of mathematics that is difficult for students to learn, challenging to teach, and critical for students' success as learners and in their future lives and careers.

Drawing on their experiences as teachers, researchers, and mathematicians, the authors have identified the big ideas that are at the heart of each book's topic. A set of essential understandings—mathematical points that capture the essence of the topic—fleshes out each big idea. Taken collectively, the big ideas and essential understandings give a view of a mathematics that is focused, connected, and useful to teachers. Links to topics that students encounter earlier and later in school mathematics and to instruction and assessment practices illustrate the relevance and importance of a teacher's essential understanding of mathematics.

On behalf of the Board of Directors, I offer sincere thanks and appreciation to everyone who has helped to make this series possible. I extend special thanks to Rose Mary Zbiek for her leadership as series editor. I join the Essential Understanding project team in welcoming you to these books and in wishing you many years of continued enjoyment of learning and teaching mathematics.

Henry Kepner
President, 2008–2010
National Council of Teachers of Mathematics

Preface

From prekindergarten through grade 12, the school mathematics curriculum includes important topics that are pivotal in students' development. Students who understand these ideas cross smoothly into new mathematical terrain and continue moving forward with assurance.

However, many of these topics have traditionally been challenging to teach as well as learn, and they often prove to be barriers rather than gateways to students' progress. Students who fail to get a solid grounding in them frequently lose momentum and struggle in subsequent work in mathematics and related disciplines.

The Essential Understanding Series identifies such topics at all levels. Teachers who engage students in these topics play critical roles in students' mathematical achievement. Each volume in the series invites teachers who aim to be not just proficient but outstanding in the classroom—teachers like you—to enrich their understanding of one or more of these topics to ensure students' continued development in mathematics.

How much do you need to know?

To teach these challenging topics effectively, you must draw on a mathematical understanding that is both broad and deep. The challenge is to know considerably more about the topic than you expect your students to know and learn.

Why does your knowledge need to be so extensive? Why must it go above and beyond what you need to teach and your students need to learn? The answer to this question has many parts.

To plan successful learning experiences, you need to understand different models and representations and, in some cases, emerging technologies as you evaluate curriculum materials and create lessons. As you choose and implement learning tasks, you need to know what to emphasize and why those ideas are mathematically important.

While engaging your students in lessons, you must anticipate their perplexities, help them avoid known pitfalls, and recognize and dispel misconceptions. You need to capitalize on unexpected classroom opportunities to make connections among mathematical ideas. If assessment shows that students have not understood the material adequately, you need to know how to address weaknesses that you have identified in their understanding. Your understanding must be sufficiently versatile to allow you to represent the mathematics in different ways to students who don't understand it the first time.

In addition, you need to know where the topic fits in the full span of the mathematics curriculum. You must understand where your students are coming from in their thinking and where they are heading mathematically in the months and years to come.

Accomplishing these tasks in mathematically sound ways is a tall order. A rich understanding of the mathematics supports the varied work of teaching as you guide your students and keep their learning on track.

How can the Essential Understanding Series help?

The Essential Understanding books offer you an opportunity to delve into the mathematics that you teach and reinforce your content knowledge. They do not include materials for you to use directly with your students, nor do they discuss classroom management, teaching styles, or assessment techniques. Instead, these books focus squarely on issues of mathematical content—the ideas and understanding that you must bring to your preparation, in-class instruction, one-on-one interactions with students, and assessment.

How do the authors approach the topics?

Big ideas and essential understandings are identified by icons in the books.

marks a big idea,

and

marks an essential understanding.

For each topic, the authors identify "big ideas" and "essential understandings." The big ideas are mathematical statements of overarching concepts that are central to a mathematical topic and link numerous smaller mathematical ideas into coherent wholes. The books call the smaller, more concrete ideas that are associated with each big idea *essential understandings*. They capture aspects of the corresponding big idea and provide evidence of its richness.

The big ideas have tremendous value in mathematics. You can gain an appreciation of the power and worth of these densely packed statements through persistent work with the interrelated essential understandings. Grasping these multiple smaller concepts and through them gaining access to the big ideas can greatly increase your intellectual assets and classroom possibilities.

In your work with mathematical ideas in your role as a teacher, you have probably observed that the essential understandings are often at the heart of the understanding that you need for presenting one of these challenging topics to students. Knowing these ideas very well is critical because they are the mathematical pieces that connect to form each big idea.

How are the books organized?

Every book in the Essential Understanding Series has the same structure:

- The introduction gives an overview, explaining the reasons for the selection of the particular topic and highlighting some of the differences between what teachers and students need to know about it.

- Chapter 1 is the heart of the book, identifying and examining the big ideas and related essential understandings.
- Chapter 2 reconsiders the ideas discussed in chapter 1 in light of their connections with mathematical ideas within the grade band and with other mathematics that the students have encountered earlier or will encounter later in their study of mathematics.
- Chapter 3 wraps up the discussion by considering the challenges that students often face in grasping the necessary concepts related to the topic under discussion. It analyzes the development of their thinking and offers guidance for presenting ideas to them and assessing their understanding.

The discussion of big ideas and essential understandings in chapter 1 is interspersed with questions labeled "Reflect." It is important to pause in your reading to think about these on your own or discuss them with your colleagues. By engaging with the material in this way, you can make the experience of reading the book participatory, interactive, and dynamic.

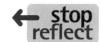

← stop reflect

marks an "Reflect" question that appears on a different page.

Reflect questions can also serve as topics of conversation among local groups of teachers or teachers connected electronically in school districts or even between states. Thus, the Reflect items can extend the possibilities for using the books as tools for formal or informal experiences for in-service and preservice teachers, individually or in groups, in or beyond college or university classes.

A new perspective

The Essential Understanding Series thus is intended to support you in gaining a deep and broad understanding of mathematics that can benefit your students in many ways. Considering connections between the mathematics under discussion and other mathematics that students encounter earlier and later in the curriculum gives the books unusual depth as well as insight into vertical articulation in school mathematics.

The series appears against the backdrop of *Principles and Standards for School Mathematics* (NCTM 2000), *Curriculum Focal Points for Prekindergarten through Grade 8 Mathematics: A Quest for Coherence* (NCTM 2006), *Focus in High School Mathematics: Reasoning and Sense Making* (NCTM 2009), and the Navigations Series (NCTM 2001–2009). The new books play an important role, supporting the work of these publications by offering content-based professional development.

The other publications, in turn, can flesh out and enrich the new books. After reading this book, for example, you might select hands-on, Standards-based activities from the Navigations books for your students to use to gain insights into the topics that the Essential Understanding books discuss. If you are teaching students in prekindergarten through grade 8, you might apply your deeper understanding as you present material related to the three focal points that *Curriculum Focal Points* identifies for instruction at your students' level. Or if you are teaching students in grades 9–12, you might use your understanding to enrich the ways in which you can engage students in mathematical reasoning and sense making as presented in *Focus in High School Mathematics*.

An enriched understanding can give you a fresh perspective and infuse new energy into your teaching. We hope that the understanding that you acquire from reading the book will support your efforts as you help your students grasp the ideas that will ensure their mathematical success.

The authors wish to thank their reviewers for their insightful contributions to this volume. They are especially grateful to Daniel Chazan and Rheta Rubenstein for their contributions.

Introduction

This book focuses on ideas about expressions, equations, and functions. These are ideas that you need to understand thoroughly and be able to use flexibly to be highly effective in your teaching of mathematics in grades 6–8. The book discusses many mathematical ideas that are common in middle school curricula, and it assumes that you have had a variety of mathematics experiences that have motivated you to delve into—and move beyond—the mathematics that you expect your students to learn.

The book is designed to engage you with these ideas, helping you to develop an understanding that will guide you in planning and implementing lessons and assessing your students' learning in ways that reflect the full complexity of expressions, equations, and functions. A deep, rich understanding of ideas about these concepts will enable you to communicate their influence and scope to your students, showing them how these ideas permeate the mathematics that they have encountered—and will continue to encounter—throughout their school mathematics experiences.

The understanding of expressions, equations, and functions that you gain from this focused study thus supports the vision of *Principles and Standards for School Mathematics* (NCTM 2000): "Imagine a classroom, a school, or a school district where all students have access to high-quality, engaging mathematics instruction" (p. 3). This vision depends on classroom teachers who "are continually growing as professionals" (p. 3) and routinely engage their students in meaningful experiences that help them learn mathematics with understanding.

Why Expressions, Equations, and Functions?

Like the topics of all the volumes in NCTM's Essential Understanding Series, expressions, equations, and functions compose a major area of school mathematics that is crucial for students to learn but challenging for teachers to teach. Students in grades 6–8 need to understand algebraic ideas well if they are to succeed in these grades and in their subsequent mathematics experiences. Learners often struggle with ideas about expressions, equations, and functions. Why do some equations have one solution, others two or even more solutions, and some no solutions? The importance of understanding how the properties of equality can be used in different orders and the challenge of transforming expressions and equations fluently make it essential for teachers of grades 6–8 to understand expressions, equations, and functions extremely well themselves.

Your work as a teacher of mathematics in these grades calls for a solid understanding of the mathematics that you—and your school, your district, and your state curriculum—expect your students to learn about expressions, equations, and functions. Your work also requires you to know how this mathematics relates to other mathematical ideas that your students will encounter in the lesson at hand, the current school year, and beyond. Rich mathematical understanding guides teachers' decisions in much of their work, such as choosing tasks for a lesson, posing questions, selecting materials, ordering topics and ideas over time, assessing the quality of students' work, and devising ways to challenge and support their thinking.

Understanding Expressions, Equations, and Functions

Teachers teach mathematics because they want others to understand it in ways that will contribute to success and satisfaction in school, work, and life. Helping your students develop a robust and lasting understanding of expressions, equations, and functions requires that you understand this mathematics deeply. But what does this mean?

It is easy to think that understanding an area of mathematics, such as expressions, equations, and functions, means knowing certain facts, being able to solve particular types of problems, and mastering relevant vocabulary. For example, as a teacher in the middle grades, you are expected to know with certainty that the same number can be added to both sides of an equation without affecting the equivalence of the expressions on either side of the equals sign. You are also expected to be skillful in solving linear equations and inequalities. Your mathematical vocabulary is assumed to include such terms as *variable*, *solution*, *domain*, *quadratic formula*, and *rate of change*.

Obviously, facts, vocabulary, and techniques for solving certain types of problems are not all that you are expected to know about expressions, equations, and functions. For example, in your ongoing work with students, you have undoubtedly discovered that you need not only to know common techniques for solving linear questions but also to be able to follow strategies that your students create.

It is also easy to focus on a very long list of mathematical ideas that all teachers of mathematics in grades 6–8 are expected to know and teach about expressions, equations, and functions. Curriculum developers often devise and publish such lists. However important the individual items might be, these lists cannot capture the essence of a rich understanding of the topic. Understanding expressions, equations, and functions deeply requires you not only to know important mathematical ideas but also to recognize how these ideas relate to one another. Your understanding continues to grow with experience and as a result of opportunities to embrace new ideas and find new connections among familiar ones.

Furthermore, your understanding of expressions, equations, and functions should transcend the content intended for your students. Some of the differences between what you need to know and what you expect them to learn are easy to point out. For instance, your understanding of the topic should include a grasp of procedures for solving logarithmic and exponential equations—mathematics that your students will encounter later but do not yet understand.

Other differences between the understanding that you need to have and the understanding that you expect your students to acquire are less obvious, but your experiences in the classroom have undoubtedly made you aware of them at some level. For example, how many times have you been grateful to have an understanding of expressions, equations, and functions that enables you to recognize the merit in a student's unanticipated mathematical question or claim? How many other times have you wondered whether you could be missing such an opportunity or failing to use it to full advantage because of a gap in your knowledge?

As you have almost certainly discovered, knowing and being able to do familiar mathematics are not enough when you're in the classroom. You also need to be able to identify and justify or refute novel claims. These claims and justifications might draw on ideas or techniques that are beyond the mathematical experiences of your students and current curricular expectations for them. For example, you may need to be able to refute the often-asserted, erroneous claim that a function is an equation. Or you may need to explain to a student why we sometimes need to "switch" the direction of an inequality symbol.

Big Ideas and Essential Understandings

Thinking about the many particular ideas that are part of a rich understanding of expressions, equations, and functions can be an overwhelming task. Articulating all of those mathematical ideas and their connections would require many books. To choose which ideas to include in this book, the authors considered a critical question: What is *essential* for teachers of mathematics in grades 6–8 to know about expressions, equations, and functions to be effective in the classroom? To answer this question, the authors drew on a variety of resources, including personal experiences, the expertise of colleagues in mathematics and mathematics education, and the reactions of reviewers and professional development providers, as well as ideas from curricular materials and research on mathematics learning and teaching.

As a result, the mathematical content of this book focuses on essential ideas for teachers about expressions, equations, and functions. In particular, chapter 1 is organized around five big ideas related to this important area of mathematics. Each big idea is supported by smaller, more specific mathematical ideas, which the book calls *essential understandings*.

Benefits for Teaching, Learning, and Assessing

Understanding expressions, equations, and functions can help you implement the Teaching Principle enunciated in *Principles and Standards for School Mathematics*. This Principle sets a high standard for instruction: "Effective mathematics teaching requires understanding what students know and need to learn and then challenging and supporting them to learn it well" (NCTM 2000, p. 16). As in teaching about other critical topics in mathematics, teaching about expressions, equations, and functions requires knowledge that goes "beyond what most teachers experience in standard preservice mathematics courses" (p. 17).

Chapter 1 comes into play at this point, offering an overview of the topic that is intended to be more focused and comprehensive than many discussions that you are likely to have encountered. This chapter enumerates, expands on, and gives examples of the big ideas and essential understandings related to expressions, equations, and functions, with the goal of supplementing or reinforcing your understanding. Thus, chapter 1 aims to prepare you to implement the Teaching Principle fully as you provide the support and challenge that your students need for robust learning about expressions, equations, and functions.

Consolidating your understanding in this way also prepares you to implement the Learning Principle outlined in *Principles and Standards*: "Students must learn mathematics with understanding, actively building new knowledge from experience and prior knowledge" (NCTM 2000, p. 20). To support your efforts to help your students learn about the concepts in this way, chapter 2 builds on the understanding of these operations that chapter 1 communicates by pointing out specific ways in which the big ideas and essential understandings connect with mathematics that students typically encounter earlier or later in school. This chapter supports the Learning Principle by emphasizing longitudinal connections in students' learning about expressions, equations, and functions. For example, as their mathematical experiences expand, students gradually develop an understanding of how the solution methods that they use with linear equations have parallels in methods for solving other types of equations, and they become fluent in using different approaches to solve equations.

The understanding that chapters 1 and 2 convey can strengthen another critical area of teaching. Chapter 3 addresses this area, building on the first two chapters to show how an understanding of expressions, equations, and functions can help you select and develop appropriate tasks, techniques, and tools for assessing your students' understanding of expressions, equations, and functions. An ownership of the big ideas and essential understandings related to expressions, equations, and functions, reinforced by an understanding of students' past and future experiences with related ideas, can help you ensure that assessment in your classroom supports the learning of significant mathematics.

Such assessment satisfies the first requirement of the Assessment Principle set out in *Principles and Standards*: "Assessment should support the learning of important mathematics and furnish useful information to both teachers and students" (NCTM 2000, p. 22). An understanding of expressions, equations, and functions can also help you satisfy the second requirement of the Assessment Principle, by enabling you to develop assessment tasks that give you specific information about what your students are thinking and what they understand. For example, you might ask students to decide whether the values in the table in figure 0.1 represent a linear pattern. Would they be able to explain that the values do not represent a linear pattern, because the change in the perimeter is not constant for each unit of change in the number of the term in the pattern?

Term in a pattern	Perimeter of the shape (cm)
1	0
3	10
4	20
6	30

Fig. 0.1. A table showing the perimeters of shapes in a growing pattern

Ready to Begin

This introduction has painted the background, preparing you for the big ideas and associated essential understandings related to expressions, equations, and functions that you will encounter and explore in chapter 1. Reading the chapters in the order in which they appear can be a very useful way to approach the book. Read chapter 1 in more than one sitting, allowing time for reflection. Take time also to use a graphing calculator or other mathematical tools with items that recommend technology use. Absorb the ideas—both big ideas and essential understandings—related to expressions, equations, and functions. Appreciate the connections among these ideas. Carry your newfound or reinforced understanding to chapter 2, which guides you in seeing how the ideas related to expressions, equations, and functions are connected to the mathematics that your students have encountered earlier or will encounter later in school. Then read about teaching, learning, and assessment issues in chapter 3.

Alternatively, you may want to take a look at chapter 3 before engaging with the mathematical ideas in chapters 1 and 2. Having the challenges of teaching, learning, and assessment issues clearly in mind, along with possible approaches to them, can give you a different perspective on the material in the earlier chapters.

No matter how you read the book, let it serve as a tool to expand your understanding, application, and enjoyment of expressions, equations, and functions.

Chapter

1

Expressions, Equations, and Functions: The Big Ideas and Essential Understandings

This book explores essential understandings about expressions, equations, and functions for teaching mathematics in grades 6–8. As a way to explore these mathematical ideas, we anchor our discussion in a familiar context. Many middle school teachers are asked to take on extra responsibilities as advisers to student groups and clubs in their schools. Imagine that you have been asked to advise a student service club during the school year. Part of your role as advisor is to help the students choose local charities for the club to support, and then to assist the students in planning and implementing fundraisers for these organizations. Suppose that you and your students have decided to plan a fundraiser each quarter, and you have selected as your four events a 5K run, a dance-a-thon, an intramural soccer game, and a T-shirt sale. Reflect 1.1 invites you to think about the variety of mathematical quantities, expressions, and relationships that might be involved in these fundraising situations.

Reflect 1.1

Suppose that you are advising a student service club that is planning four fundraisers: a 5K run, a dance-a-thon, a soccer game, and a T-shirt sale. What *quantities* might you and your student club members think about for each of these fundraisers? What are some *mathematical expressions* that might help in reasoning about aspects of these fundraisers? What *relationships between quantities* might require investigation?

In planning a 5K run, for example, some quantities to think about would be the number of participants, the rate at which the participants are likely to run, and the amount of money that each runner might be able to collect. For the T-shirt sale, you and the club members might consider expenditures for purchasing the T-shirts and having them printed, and then you might weigh these costs against the expected profit, depending on how much the club members charge for the T-shirts at the sale. Planning the soccer game would involve considering the number of tickets that club members might sell, how much they might charge for adults and children, and so on. In many of these cases, *profit* is a quantity that links the number of items sold (the number of T-shirts or soccer game tickets) to the amount of money the group might earn for their charities. As we will explore later, students in the club might, for example, purchase T-shirts for \$5 each and pay an additional \$3 apiece for silk screening. If x represents the number of T-shirts purchased, then the expression $8x$ can represent the club's corresponding expenditures in dollars.

These examples place us squarely in the realm of algebra. Algebra is an important area of mathematics that provides concepts and tools that allow us to describe, analyze, and understand many situations and relationships, both in mathematics and in the real world. This book explores five big ideas in algebra that are particularly relevant to the teaching of mathematics in grades 6–8. The book's intended audience is middle school mathematics teachers, and its focus is on providing teachers with experiences that will allow them to explore and discuss the five big ideas. Although the mathematics that teachers need to know overlaps the mathematics that students need to learn, this book does not present a set of curricular standards such as those set forth in *Principles and Standards for School Mathematics* (NCTM 2000), the Common Core State Standards for Mathematics (Common Core State Standards Initiative [CCSSI] 2010), or state and district standards. Rather, it offers opportunities for you to "unpack" five big ideas and develop deeper, more interconnected understandings of expressions, equations, and functions so that you can support students' learning about these important mathematical ideas:

Big Idea 1. Expressions. Expressions are foundational for algebra; they serve as building blocks for work with equations and functions.

Big Idea 2. Variables. Variables are tools for expressing mathematical ideas clearly and concisely. They have many different meanings, depending on context and purpose.

Big Idea 3. Equality. The equals sign indicates that two expressions are equivalent. It can also be used in defining or naming a single expression or function rule.

Big Idea 4. Representing and analyzing functions. Functions provide a means for describing and understanding relationships between variables. They can have multiple representations—in algebraic symbols, situations, graphs, verbal descriptions, tables, and so on—and they can be classified into different *families* with similar patterns of change.

Big Idea 5. Solving equations. General algorithms exist for solving many kinds of equations; these algorithms are broadly applicable for solving a wide range of similar equations. However, for some problems or situations, alternatives to these general algorithms may be more elegant, efficient, or informative.

Note the use of the word *situation* in Big Ideas 4 and 5. In this book, *situations* include both experientially "real" circumstances that students explore concretely and immediately (for example, by working with algebra tiles) and circumstances in stated problems that are based on situations from everyday life.

Each of the five big ideas listed above is supported by a number of "essential understandings." By exploring and grasping the related essential understandings, we can develop a rich and coherent sense of each big idea.

Big Idea 1. Expressions

Essential Understanding 1*a*. Expressions are powerful tools for exploring, reasoning about, and representing situations.

Essential Understanding 1*b*. Two or more expressions may be equivalent, even when their symbolic forms differ.

Essential Understanding 1*c*. A relatively small number of symbolic transformations can be applied to expressions to yield equivalent expressions.

Big Idea 2. Variables

Essential Understanding 2*a*. Variables have many different meanings, depending on context and purpose.

Essential Understanding 2*b*. Using variables permits writing expressions whose values are not known or vary under different circumstances.

Essential Understanding 2*c*. Using variables permits representing varying quantities. This use of variables is particularly important in studying relationships between varying quantities.

Big Idea 3. Equality

Essential Understanding 3*a*. The equals sign can indicate that two expressions are equivalent.

Essential Understanding 3*b*. The equals sign can be used in defining or giving a name to an expression or function rule.

Essential Understanding 3c. It is often important to find the value(s) of a variable for which two expressions represent the same quantity.

Essential Understanding 3*d*. Finding the value(s) of a variable for which two expressions represent the same quantity is known as *solving an equation.*

Essential Understanding 3e. An inequality is another way to describe a relationship between expressions; instead of showing that the values of two expressions are equal, inequalities indicate that the value of one expression is greater than (or greater than or equal to) the value of the other expression.

Essential Understanding 3*f*. In solving an inequality, multiplying or dividing both expressions by a negative number reverses the sign ($<$, $>$, $\leq$, $\geq$) that indicates the relationship between the two expressions.

Big Idea 4. Representing and analyzing functions

Essential Understanding 4*a*. Functions provide a tool for describing how variables change together. Using a function in this way is called *modeling*, and the function is called a *model.*

Essential Understanding 4*b*. Functions can be represented in multiple ways—in algebraic symbols, situations, graphs, verbal descriptions, tables, and so on—and these representations, and the links among them, are useful in analyzing patterns of change.

Essential Understanding 4c. One important way of describing functions is by identifying the rate at which the variables change together. It is useful to group functions into *families* with similar patterns of change because these functions, and the situations that they model, share certain general characteristics.

Essential Understanding 4*d*. Some representations of a function may be more useful than others, depending on how they are used.

Essential Understanding 4*e*. Linear functions have constant rates of change.

Essential Understanding 4*f*. Quadratic functions are characterized by rates of change that change at a constant rate.

Essential Understanding 4*g*. In exponential growth, the rate of change increases over the domain, but in exponential decay, the rate of change decreases over the domain.

Big Idea 5. Solving equations

Essential Understanding 5*a*. A general algorithm exists for solving linear equations. This algorithm is broadly applicable and reasonably efficient.

Essential Understanding 5*b*. Linear equations can be solved by symbolic, graphical, and numerical methods. On some occasions and in some contexts, one solution method may be more elegant, efficient, or informative than another.

Essential Understanding 5*c*. Quadratic equations can be solved by using graphs and tables and by applying an algorithm that involves *completing the square*. This algorithm, when expressed in a more compact form, is also known as the *quadratic formula*.

These big ideas and essential understandings are identified here to give you a quick overview and for your convenience in referring back to them later. The chapter will discuss each one in turn in detail.

Expressions as Building Blocks: Big Idea 1

Big Idea 1. *Expressions are foundational for algebra; they serve as building blocks for work with equations and functions.*

An algebraic *expression* is a mathematical phrase made up of one or more numbers or variables or operations on them. An expression represents a quantity, which is known as the *value* of the expression. Reflect 1.2 encourages you to begin thinking about the ways that you and your students work with expressions in middle school mathematics classes.

Reflect 1.2

What kinds of expressions do your students work with in your mathematics class? How are expressions in elementary school different from expressions in middle school?

Sometimes an expression clearly indicates a number, such as the expression 4 or 5 + 3. In other cases, an expression may represent a quantity whose numerical value is not known, such as the expression $2x$, $7x + 2y$, or $4a - 7$. Many students enter middle school having worked primarily with numerical expressions. In algebra, expressions are powerful tools for representing and analyzing relationships more generally, and this work is fundamentally what algebra is all about.

Exploring, reasoning about, and representing situations

Essential Understanding 1a. *Expressions are powerful tools for exploring, reasoning about, and representing situations.*

Returning to the hypothetical context of the student service club, consider expressions that you, as advisor, and your club members might write for use in exploring and reasoning about one of your upcoming fundraisers—a T-shirt sale. Imagine that the club can buy T-shirts for $4 each, and (since this is a fundraiser) the members plan to sell the shirts for $10 each. Let x stand for the number of T-shirts that the club sells at the T-shirt sale. The expression $4x$ could then stand for the cost in dollars of purchasing x T-shirts, and the expression $10x$ could stand for the amount of money in dollars that the club would take in from selling x T-shirts. How might these expressions be useful in understanding this situation? Reflect 1.3 asks you to consider this question.

Reflect 1.3

Suppose that in planning a T-shirt fundraiser, you and the students in your service club use the expression $4x$ to stand for the cost, in dollars, that the club must spend to purchase x T-shirts and the expression $10x$ to stand for the amount, in dollars, that the club will take in from selling the shirts. How might you and the club members represent these different expressions to understand the situation better, including how much money the club might spend and take in from the T-shirt sale?

You and the students in your club could explore this situation by displaying these expressions in various representations, particularly graphs and tables. For example, the table in figure 1.1 shows the purchase cost and the money that the club would receive from the sale of various numbers of T-shirts.

x (number of T-shirts sold)	$4x$ (cost, in dollars, of purchasing x T-shirts)	$10x$ (amount, in dollars, received from selling x T-shirts)
1	4(1), or $4	10(1), or $10
5	4(5), or $20	10(5), or $50
50	4(50), or $200	10(50), or $500
100	4(100), or $400	10(100), or $1000

Fig. 1.1. The purchase cost and money received from the sale of various numbers of T-shirts purchased for $4 each and sold for $10 each

You could also graph these expressions as another way to explore the situation. For example, the graph in figure 1.2 shows the ordered pairs $(x, 4x)$, with the horizontal axis representing the number of T-shirts that the club purchases and the vertical axis representing the cost of purchasing x T-shirts.

Graphs are particularly useful for exploring mathematical features of situations such as this one. You and the members of your club could make a number of observations on the basis of this graph. First, the point (0, 0) is on the graph, so purchasing zero T-shirts costs $0. Second, no points are plotted for negative values of x; in the T-shirt sale context, purchasing negative numbers of T-shirts does not make sense. Third, for each additional T-shirt purchased, the total cost increases by a constant amount, which is $4. In Reflect 1.4, consider how you might write different expressions for the club's profit in the T-shirt sale.

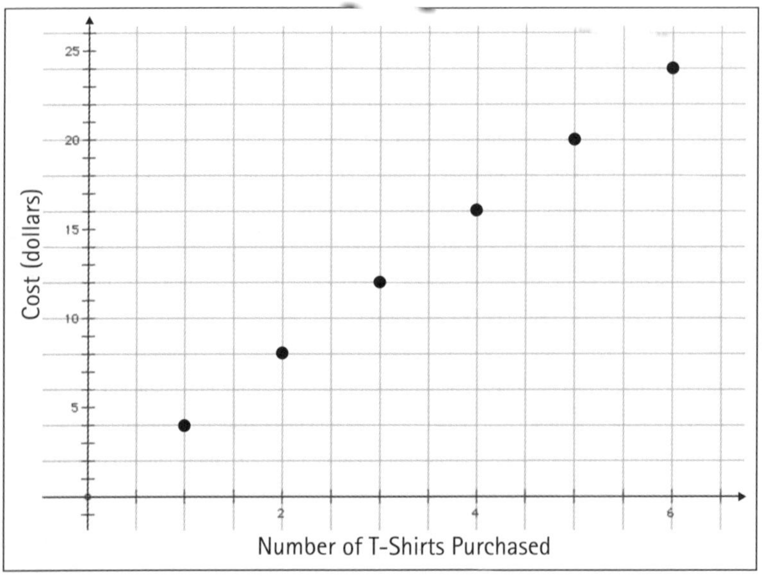

Fig. 1.2. A graph of the relationship between the number of T-shirts purchased and the cost (at $4 for each T-shirt)

Reflect 1.4

In planning the T-shirt sale, you and the students in your service club could write your expected profit as $10x - 4x$ or as $6x$. Explain what each of these expressions would mean and why each expression would make sense in the context.

Note that for a single context, we can often write many different expressions that are equivalent. Let's consider expressions for describing the service club's profit for selling x T-shirts at the T-shirt sale. One way to consider profit would be to take the total revenue (how much money the club will take in at the T-shirt sale) and subtract the total expenditure (how much money the club has to spend to purchase the T-shirts). If the revenue is $10x$ and the expenditure is $4x$, then we can write the expression $10x - 4x$ to represent the club's profit. Another, equivalent way to think about the profit is to consider that if each T-shirt costs the club $4 and is sold for $10, the club makes a profit of $6 for every T-shirt that it sells. If the club sells x T-shirts, an expression that we can write for its profit is $6x$. Thus, by reasoning through this context, we have generated two different expressions for the profit: $10x - 4x$ and $6x$.

Equivalent expressions

Essential Understanding 1b. *Two or more expressions may be equivalent, even when their symbolic forms differ.*

Two or more expressions are called *equivalent* if they have the same value, regardless of what number is consistently substituted for all instances of a particular variable. In the example of the hypothetical service club that is planning a T-shirt sale as a fundraiser, we were able to reason about the context to write two different but equivalent expressions for profit, $10x - 4x$, and $6x$, for all whole numbers x. Even though these two expressions have different symbolic forms, they represent the same quantity when each variable in both expressions has the same value. In such a case, both expressions have the same value no matter how many T-shirts the service club sells, so the two expressions are equivalent. Consider Reflect 1.5, in which two expressions with different symbolic forms represent the same quantity.

The use of algebraic symbols, like any generalizing process, involves appropriate domains. See *Developing Essential Understanding of Algebraic Thinking for Teaching Mathematics in Grades 3–5* (Blanton et al. 2011) for additional discussion of domain and its role in reasoning.

Reflect 1.5

Suppose that in planning a dance-a-thon as one quarter's fundraiser, your service club members decide to set up tables where participants can rest and enjoy refreshments while watching the dancers. The tables will be organized in long rectangles along the walls of the dance floor, with the long rectangles made up of smaller rectangular tables. Suppose that you and your students make a diagram like that in figure 1.3 to show the arrangement of n tables, with **O** indicating a seat for a single person and "..." indicating that n varies. How many people can be seated at a table made up of n smaller rectangular tables? One way that you and your service club members might describe this situation is by writing the expression $2 \cdot 2n + 1 + 1$. Another is by writing the expression $4(n - 2) + 10$. Explain what each of these expressions means in relation to the arrangement in figure 1.3.

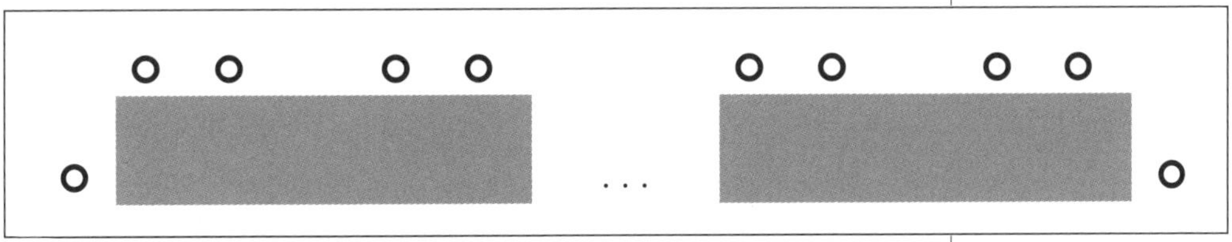

Fig. 1.3. Arrangement of tables and chairs at the dance-a-thon

You and the students in your service club might describe the situation by noticing that there are two pairs of seats facing the dance floor at each of the n tables ($2 \cdot 2n$), and there is one seat at each end of the long rectangle of tables ($1 + 1$). This thinking could lead to writing the expression $2 \cdot 2n + 1 + 1$ for the number of seats. Alternatively, you might describe the number of seats by writing the expression $4 \cdot (n - 2) + 10$ because there are $n - 2$ tables with 4 seats each, and there are a total of 10 additional seats at the two end tables. In many situations, including this one, there are different ways to write an expression, depending on how one thinks about the situation. This notion is expressed in Essential Understanding 1*b*.

It is often important to determine whether two or more expressions are equivalent. Many times, equivalence or nonequivalence is not immediately clear. In such cases, there are a number of ways to determine whether two expressions have the same value when any variable that appears in both has the same value in every appearance. Sometimes (as in the case of a real-world problem such as that involving the T-shirt profit), it is possible to reason about the context to determine whether two or more expressions are equivalent. However, in other cases, determining the equivalence of two expressions is not so straightforward. Yet, even in these circumstances, we can investigate whether two expressions are equivalent in a number of ways.

First, we can substitute the same value for the each instance of a particular variable in each expression and see if both expressions yield the same quantity. For example, let's continue to consider the expressions $10x - 4x$ and $6x$. One way to explore whether these are equivalent expressions is to make a table and substitute values for x in each expression, as shown in the table in figure 1.4. Because both expressions appear to have the same value for each value of the variable x, we might conjecture that these two expressions are equivalent.

Value of x	Value of expression $10x - 4x$	Value of expression $6x$
0	10(0) – 4(0), or 0	6(0), or 0
1	10(1) – 4(1), or 6	6(1), or 6
2	10(2) – 4(2), or 12	6(2), or 12
3	10(3) – 4(3), or 18	6(3), or 18

Fig. 1.4. Values of the expressions $10x - 4x$ and $6x$ for a few values of the variable x

Let's consider another example—one that does not give us a real-world context about which to reason. Consider the expressions $3(x + 4)$ and $3x + 12$ and the table shown in figure 1.5. As in the previous example, because both expressions have the same value when x has the same value in both, we might conjecture that these two expressions are equivalent.

Value of x	Value of expression $3(x + 4)$	Value of expression $3x + 12$
0	3(0 + 4), or 12	3(0) + 12, or 12
1	3(1 + 4), or 15	3(1) + 12, or 15
2	3(2 + 4), or 18	3(2) + 12, or 18
3	3(3 + 4), or 21	3(3) + 12, or 21

Fig. 1.5. Values of the expressions $3(x + 4)$ and $3x + 12$ for a few values of the variable x

It is important to note that two such expressions are equivalent only if they have the same value for *all* values of the variable x. In the two examples above, the expressions have the same value when x is 0, 1, 2, or 3. But is this true for all other values of x? In some cases, two expressions may appear to represent the same quantity when the same value is substituted for a variable that appears in both, but more thorough investigation reveals that the expressions represent different quantities for other values of the variables.

For example, imagine that your service club has decided to combine fundraisers by selling T-shirts at the soccer game. Suppose that tickets to the soccer game cost \$2 for a child and \$5 for an adult, and T-shirts cost \$10 each. You might again let x stand for the number of T-shirts sold while letting y stand for the number of children and z stand for the number of adults who buy tickets to the soccer game. So you could represent the revenue from selling tickets to the game as $2y + 5z$. How would the revenue from selling soccer game tickets $(2y + 5z)$ relate to the revenue from selling T-shirts $(10x)$? Reflect 1.6 asks you to explore the values of these two expressions for various values of the variables x, y, and z.

Reflect 1.6

What are some values of x, y, and z that make the expressions $2y + 5z$ and $10x$ represent the same amount of revenue? Are there other values of x, y, and z that you can find to make the expressions produce different revenues?

Consider the table in figure 1.6. As this table indicates, there are many values of x, y, and z for which these two expressions have the same value. So, it might appear that $2y + 5z$ and $10x$ are equivalent expressions.

Now consider the table in figure 1.7. For other values of x, y, and z, this table indicates that these two expressions do not have the same value.

Value of x	Value of y	Value of z	Value of expression $10x$	Value of expression $2y + 5z$
0	0	0	10(0), or 0	2(0) + 5(0), or 0
1	0	2	10(1), or 10	2(0) + 5(2), or 10
2	10	0	10(2), or 20	2(10) + 5(0), or 20
3	15	0	10(3), or 30	2(15) + 5(0), or 30

Fig. 1.6. Values of the expressions $10x$ and $2y + 5z$ for a few values of x, y, and z

Value of x	Value of y	Value of z	Value of expression $10x$	Value of expression $2y + 5z$
0	0	1	10(0), or 0	2(0) + 5(1), or 5
1	1	1	10(1), or 10	2(1) + 5(1), or 7
2	1	2	10(2), or 20	2(1) + 5(2), or 12
3	2	3	10(3), or 30	2(2) + 5(3), or 19

Fig. 1.7. Values of the expressions $10x$ and $2y + 5z$ for a few more values of x, y, and z

For an example that is unrelated to our hypothetical service club context, consider the expressions $x - 2$ and $|x - 2|$. As the table in figure 1.8 suggests, these expressions have the same value for all values of x that are greater than or equal to 2, but they have different values for all values of x that are less than 2.

Value of x	Value of expression $x - 2$	Value of expression $|x - 2|$
-2	-2 - 2, or -4	|-2 - 2|, or 4
-1	-1 - 2, or -3	|-1 - 2|, or 3
0	0 - 2, or -2	|0 - 2|, or 2
1	1 - 2, or -1	|1 - 2|, or 1
2	2 - 2, or 0	|2 - 2|, or 0
3	3 - 2, or 1	|3 - 2|, or 1
4	4 - 2, or 2	|4 - 2|, or 2
5	5 - 2, or 3	|5 - 2|, or 3

Fig. 1.8. The values of the expressions $x - 2$ and $|x - 2|$ for a few values of the variable x

By carefully choosing values to substitute for the variables in each expression, we may become reasonably confident about the equivalence of two expressions. Yet, it is clearly impossible to make a table to check the values of the expressions for *all* values of the variables. As a result, this method of exploring the equivalence of two expressions should be used with caution.

Another way to probe the equivalence of two expressions is to construct a graph. In middle school, this method is most applicable to expressions containing a single variable. For example, consider the earlier example of the two expressions for profit from the T-shirt sale: $10x - 4x$ and $6x$. For each expression, students could plot an ordered pair $(x, 10x - 4x)$ or $(x, 6x)$ for a particular value of x and the value of the expression for this value of x. Although this method is essentially the same as making a table, it is sometimes possible to extend patterns that are indicated by the graph to gain confidence about the equivalence of the two expressions. As shown in figure 1.9, after plotting the ordered pairs (1, 6), (2, 12), (3, 18), and (4, 24), we might conjecture that these two expressions are linear, that they represent the same line, that they have the same value for all values of x, and thus that they are equivalent.

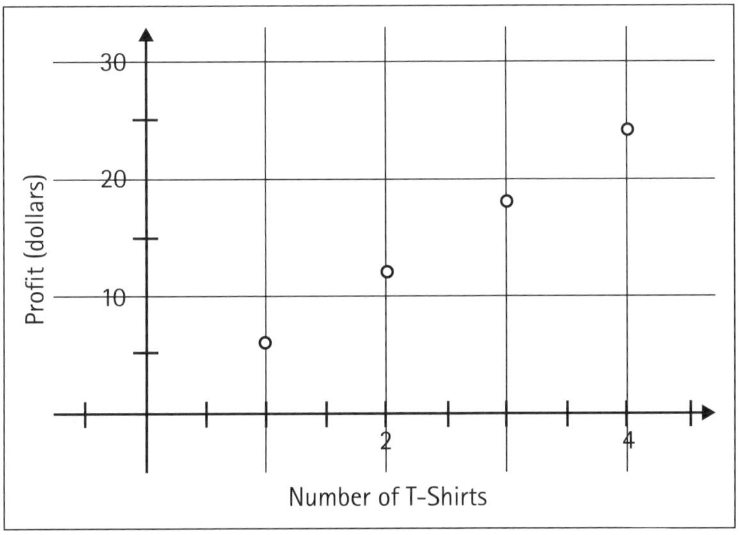

Fig. 1.9. A graph showing four ordered pairs for the expressions $10x - 4x$ and $6x$

Graphing two expressions is a useful way to explore equivalence. Graphing ordered pairs (x, value of the expression at x) for the expressions $x - 2$ and $|x - 2|$ clearly indicates that they are not equivalent, as shown in figure 1.10.

We have discussed three ways of investigating the equivalence of two expressions: (1) by reasoning about them in their particular context, (2) by comparing values for them in a table, and (3) by plotting ordered pairs for them and comparing their graphs. In addition, we can investigate whether two expressions are equivalent in a fourth way–by transforming the symbolic representation of each expression. Transforming a symbolic representation involves using mathematical properties such as the distributive property to transform, or rewrite, an expression in a different symbolic form. If we can apply properties of numbers and operations and equality to

Sometimes the word *transformation* refers to a *reflection*, *rotation*, *translation*, or other mapping in transformational geometry. Here we mean something slightly different. We are talking about a *symbolic* transformation of an expression into an equivalent expression in a different symbolic form, through the use of mathematical properties.

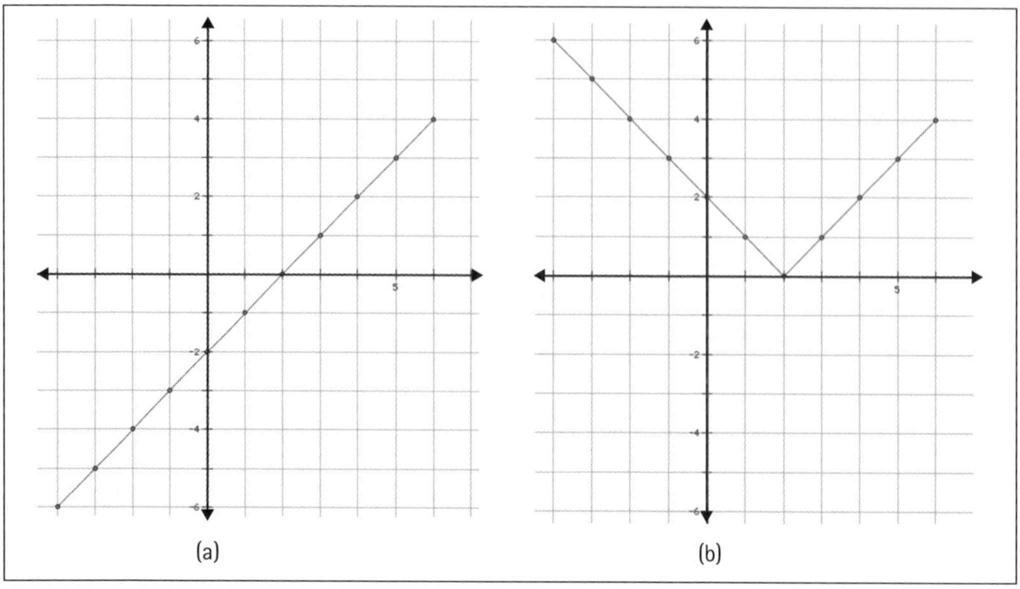

Fig. 1.10. Graphs of ordered pairs for the expressions (a) $x - 2$ and (b) $|x - 2|$

For a discussion of the distributive property of multiplication over addition in numerical contexts, see *Developing Essential Understanding of Multiplication and Division for Teaching Mathematics in Grades 3–5* (Otto et al. 2011).

transform the symbolic representation of one expression so that it is identical to a second expression, we have determined that the two expressions are equivalent.

Consider again the expressions $10x - 4x$ and $6x$, which we discussed earlier as representations of profit in the context of the hypothetical T-shirt sale. We can use the *distributive property of multiplication over addition* to rewrite the expression $10x - 4x$ as $(10 - 4)x$, which we can rewrite as $6x$. We have transformed the expression $10x - 4x$ in such a way that it is now identical in form to our second expression for profit from the T-shirt sale, $6x$. This means that $10x - 4x$ is equivalent to $6x$. Similarly, applying the distributive property to $3(x + 4)$ yields $3x + 3(4)$ or $3x + 12$, which indicates that the expressions $3(x + 4)$ and $3x + 12$ are equivalent.

Symbolic transformations and equivalent expressions

Essential Understanding 1c. *A relatively small number of symbolic transformations can be applied to expressions to yield equivalent expressions.*

In working with expressions, we can use particular symbolic transformations to produce new expressions that are equivalent to the original ones. Symbolic transformations based on certain mathematical properties, such as the distributive property, can be used to transform or rewrite an expression in a form that is symbolically different but mathematically equivalent.

Examples that we have discussed earlier illustrate some commonly used symbolic transformations, including the use of the distributive property to rewrite $3(x + 4)$ as $3x + 12$. In addition to the distributive property (which underlies combining like terms and factoring), symbolic transformations based on the *commutative properties of addition and multiplication* also produce expressions that are equivalent to the original ones. These symbolic transformations change the way a symbolic expression looks, but—because of the mathematical properties that underlie these transformations—they do not change the value of the expression.

Two other symbolic transformations that produce expressions that are equivalent to the original ones make use of the *multiplicative identity* and *additive identity*. These symbolic transformations are useful for transforming expressions. Reflect 1.7 focuses attention on these two symbolic transformations and your students' previous work with them.

A discussion of transformations in geometric settings appears in *Developing Essential Understanding of Geometry for Teaching Mathematics in Grades 6–8* (Sinclair, Pimm, and Skelin, forthcoming).

Reflect 1.7

What is the multiplicative identity property? What is the additive identity property? In what ways have your students used these identities before taking algebra or prealgebra?

When we multiply a number by 1 or multiply 1 by that number, the result is the number itself, so 1 is the multiplicative identity. Similarly, when we add 0 to a number or add a number to 0, the result is the number itself, so 0 is the additive identity. Although we often think of the multiplicative identity as applying mostly to numbers (for example, $5 \cdot 1$ is 5, or $^2/_3 \cdot {}^2/_2 = {}^4/_6$ when finding common denominators), it applies to algebraic expressions as well. The expression $5x$ is equivalent to the expression $5x \cdot 1$. Furthermore, for expressions with more than one term, multiplying some or all of the terms by 1 produces expressions that are equivalent to the original ones. For example, the expression $2x + 3$ is equivalent to $2x(1) + 3$, $2x + 3(1)$, $2x(1) + 3(1)$, and $(2x + 3)(1)$.

Of particular importance are the different ways in which the number 1 can be written. Because $^3/_3$ is equivalent to 1, we can multiply an expression by $^3/_3$ and produce an expression that is equivalent to our original expression. For example, the expression $2x$ is equivalent to the expression $2x \cdot {}^3/_3$, which can be rewritten as $^{6x}/_3$. In working with an expression with multiple terms, we can multiply each term by 1 in a different form and produce new expressions that are equivalent to our original expression. For example, the expression $2x + 3y$ is equivalent to

$$2x \cdot \frac{3}{3} + 3y \cdot \frac{2}{2},$$

which can be rewritten as

$$\frac{6x}{3}+\frac{6y}{2}.$$

Clever use of the multiplicative identity can transform expressions into equivalent ones. Let's revisit the previous example, where we began by saying that $2x + 3y$ is equivalent to

$$2x\cdot\frac{3}{3}+3y\cdot\frac{2}{2},$$

which we rewrote as

$$\frac{6x}{3}+\frac{6y}{2}.$$

We can transform this expression by rewriting each term with a common denominator of 6, again applying the multiplicative identity:

$$\frac{6x}{3}\cdot\frac{2}{2}+\frac{6y}{2}\cdot\frac{3}{3}$$

$$\frac{12x}{6}+\frac{18y}{6}$$

$$\frac{12x+18y}{6}$$

We can transform the expression $2x/3 + 5x/2$ into an equivalent expression in the same way:

$$\frac{2x}{3}\cdot\frac{2}{2}+\frac{5x}{2}\cdot\frac{3}{3}$$

This can be rewritten as

$$\frac{4x}{6}+\frac{15x}{6},$$

which can be rewritten as $19x/6$ by using the distributive property and combining like terms:

$$\frac{4x}{6}+\frac{15x}{6}=\left(\frac{1}{6}\cdot 4x\right)+\left(\frac{1}{6}\cdot 15x\right)=\frac{1}{6}(4x+15x)=\frac{1}{6}(19x)=\frac{19x}{6}$$

Finally, addition of 0 (which is the additive identity) is a symbolic transformation that ensures equivalence between expressions before and after the transformation. Prior to their study of algebra, students learn that $0 + 3$ is 3. As with the multiplicative identity, this symbolic transformation can also be applied to expressions; for example, $3x + 0$ is equivalent to $3x$. Reflect 1.8 offers an opportunity to explore how the additive identity can be used to transform expressions into other, equivalent expressions.

Reflect 1.8

Can you come up with at least ten different numerical expressions that can be subtracted from three to get zero? Be creative!

The number 0 can be written in infinitely many ways! For example, 3 – 3, 3 – 2 – 1, and 3 + 4 – 3 – 4 are all equivalent to 0. So, we can add (3 – 3), (3 – 2 – 1), or (3 + 4 – 3 – 4) to an expression and preserve equivalence between expressions before and after our transformations. Clever addition of different forms of 0 can be quite helpful in transforming expressions into other equivalent expressions that have different symbolic forms. For example, as we will see later in the discussion of Essential Understanding 5c, the expression $x^2 + 6x$ can be rewritten as the equivalent $x^2 + 6x + (9 - 9)$, which can be rewritten as $(x^2 + 6x + 9) - 9$, or $(x + 3)^2 - 9$. In fact, transforming one expression into another to produce an equivalent expression is often a critical step in solving a problem.

The table in figure 1.11 provides a list of transformations that ensure equivalence between the expressions that they produce and the original expressions. Reflect 1.9 probes whether any other symbolic transformations ensure equivalence.

Essential Understanding 5c *Quadratic equations can be solved by using graphs and tables and by applying an algorithm that involves* completing the square. *This algorithm, when expressed in a more compact form, is also known as the* quadratic formula.

Transformation	Sample expression	Result of application of transformation to yield an equivalent expression
Distributive property	$3(x + 4)$	$3x + 12$
Combining like terms	$10x - 4x$	$6x$
Factoring	$6x + 10y$	$2(3x + 5y)$
Commutative property of addition	$3x + 4y$	$4y + 3x$
Commutative property of multiplication	$(3x)(2y)$	$(2y)(3x)$
Multiplication by 1	$\frac{2x}{3} + \frac{5x}{2}$	$\frac{2x}{3}\left(\frac{2}{2}\right) + \frac{5x}{2}\left(\frac{3}{3}\right)$
Associative property of addition	$(x + 2) + y$	$x + (2 + y)$
Associative property of multiplication	$\frac{1}{2}(bh)$	$\left(\frac{1}{2}b\right)h$
Addition of 0	$x^2 + 6x$	$x^2 + 6x + 9 + (-9)$

Fig. 1.11. Symbolic transformations that preserve equivalence between the original expression and the expression produced

Reflect 1.9

Consider other symbolic transformations that are not included in figure 1.11, such as adding a constant to an expression. Will those transformations result in expressions that are equivalent to the original expressions?

Many types of symbolic transformations are not included in the table in figure 1.11 because they do not produce expressions that are equivalent to the original expressions. For example, adding a nonzero constant to an expression or multiplying an expression by a constant other than 1 does not produce an expression that is equivalent to the original expression; $3x$ is not equivalent to $3x + 2$, and $4x$ is not equivalent to $1/4 \cdot 4x$. Similarly, squaring or taking the square root of an expression that does not represent 0 or 1 does not produce an equivalent expression. The symbolic transformations identified in the table result in expressions that preserve equivalence with the original expressions.

Variables as Useful Tools: Big Idea 2

Big Idea 2. *Variables are tools for expressing mathematical ideas clearly and concisely. They have many different meanings, depending on context and purpose.*

The idea of variable is central to algebra. Understanding algebra requires knowing what variables are and using them as tools to indicate relationships.

Variables have many meanings

Essential Understanding 2a. *Variables have many different meanings, depending on context and purpose.*

Schoenfeld and Arcavi (1988) describe the concept of variable as "the basis for the transition from arithmetic to algebra" (p. 420). Although students work with many algebraic situations and ideas in the elementary grades, many students encounter the term *variable* for the first time in middle school. Many of the expressions that we have discussed involve variables. In the expression $4x$, which we used to describe the cost in dollars for our hypothetical service club to purchase x T-shirts for a fundraiser, the letter x is a variable representing the number of T-shirts purchased. In the expression $2y + 5z$, we used y and z as variables representing the number of children (y) and the number of adults (z) who buy tickets for the soccer game that the club is planning as another fundraiser.

The table in figure 1.12 offers examples of how several different textbooks introduce the term *variable* to students. After reading these examples, spend some time thinking about Reflect 1.10 and discussing it with colleagues, if possible.

Reflect 1.10

Consider the different presentations of *variable* in figure 1.12.

What are some similarities and differences in these various treatments of the term *variable*?

How do these ways of introducing and using variable compare with the way variable is introduced and used in the textbook(s) in your classroom?

(1)	Adults are roughly twice as tall as they were when they were 3 years old.... This suggests a simple rule of thumb for predicting the adult height of a 3-year-old child: multiply his or her current height by 2. In the language of algebra, if *c* represents the height of a 3-year-old child, then $2 \cdot c$, or $2c$ for short, is the child's predicted height as an adult. The letter *c* is a *variable* and $2c$ is an *algebraic expression*. A **variable** is a letter or other symbol that can be replaced by any number (or other object) from a set. When numbers and variables are combined using the operations of arithmetic, the result is called an **algebraic expression**. (Brown et al. 2008, p. 6)
(2)	In the jumping jack experiment, the number of jumping jacks and the time are variables. A **variable** is a quantity that changes or *varies*. You recorded your data for the variables in a table. Another way to display your data is in a coordinate graph. A **coordinate graph** is a way to show the relationship between two variables. (Lappan et al. 2004b, p. 7)
(3)	Each decision that must be made in planning the talent show will have consequences. You can choose the price for tickets, but if you charge too much, attendance will be low. If you charge too little, you will have very little income. The situation involves **variables** such as ticket price and attendance. Variables are **quantities whose values may change or vary** according to circumstances. (Fey et al. 1995, pp. 2–3)
(4)	Algebra is a language of symbols. One symbol that is frequently used is a variable. A **variable** is a placeholder for any value. As shown above, *h* represents some *unknown number* of hours. (Malloy et al. 2005, p. 17)
(5)	There is a simpler way to describe the situation. Let the variable *x* stand for the number of people needing food and shelter at a relief camp. Here is what the camp needs for *x* people. • $(x + 10)$ beds • $(3 \cdot x)$ pounds of food per day The variable *x* stands for an unknown number. When the relief group knows the number of people at the camp, they can replace *x* with that number.... The letter *x* is a **variable**, or placeholder, for a number that you do not know. Mathematical phrases, such as $x + 10$ and $3 \cdot x$, are **expressions** that use operations to combine numbers and variables. (EDC 2009, p. 93)

Fig. 1.12. Ways in which different textbooks introduce *variable*

Variables in expressions of unknown or varying value

➜ **Essential Understanding 2*b*.** *Using variables permits writing expressions whose values are not known or vary under different circumstances.*

Expressions involving variables can help us to answer questions in a variety of situations. For example, in the hypothetical situation of the T-shirt fundraiser, we supposed that the cost to the service club members is $4 for each T-shirt purchased, and we wrote the expression $4x$ to represent the club's total expenditure for x T-shirts. The expression $4x$, whose value varies under different circumstances, can help us answer a question such as, "What is the cost, in dollars, for purchasing 3 T-shirts?" With this question, we seek information about what Chazan (2000) calls a "snapshot" of the situation. We wish to determine the cost that results from purchasing a particular number of T-shirts. In this question, we are treating the variable x as an *unknown value*. When x is 3, the cost of purchasing T-shirts is $12.

Variables for studying relationships between varying quantities

Essential Understanding 2c. *Using variables permits representing varying quantities. This use of variables is particularly important in studying relationships between varying quantities.*

We can view a variable as representing not just an *unknown* quantity but also a *varying* quantity. As stated in Essential Understanding 2c, this way of thinking about variables turns out to be particularly important when it comes to studying relationships between varying quantities, as in the case of some *functions*, like those discussed in more detail in connection with Big Idea 4. If the service club has 1000 T-shirts to sell, we can think of the variable x in the expression $4x$ as ranging over the whole numbers in the interval from 0 to 1000. (We cannot buy a negative number of T-shirts or a fractional number of T-shirts.) For every unit increase in x—or increase of 1 T-shirt—the cost increases by $4. The relationship between the number of T-shirts purchased and the cost is a linear relationship, as we saw earlier in the graph in figure 1.2.

Reflect 1.11 asks you to revisit these two views of variable—as an unknown quantity and as a varying quantity—by reexamining the ways that mathematics textbooks introduce the term *variable* in figure 1.12.

Big Idea 4

Functions provide a means for describing and understanding relationships between variables. They can have multiple representations—in algebraic symbols, situations, graphs, verbal descriptions, tables, and so on—and they can be classified into different families *with similar patterns of change.*

Reflect 1.11

Which of the two views of variable—as an unknown quantity and as a varying quantity—is more prominent in each textbook excerpt shown in figure 1.12?

Which of these illustrations and views is more consistent with the perspective on variable that you emphasize in your classroom?

Revisiting the roles of *variable*

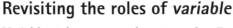

➔ Essential Understanding 2*a*
Variables have many different meanings, depending on context and purpose.

Variables take on more than two roles. Essential Understanding 2*a* states that variables have many different meanings. In fact, Usiskin (1988) identifies five conceptions of variable in algebra. The two roles described here capture perhaps the two most common and important ways that variables are used in middle school algebra.

How can we—and our students—make sense of these dual roles of variables—their capacity to represent an unknown but particular number and to take on many possible values? In an account of his own rethinking of the teaching of algebra, Chazan (2000) describes the difference between these two views as an "ambiguity or complementarity at the center of school algebra" (p. 77):

> I use the term complementarity in the same sense as it is used in describing light. Light is viewed at one and the same time as both particle and wave. Our understanding of light as a phenomenon is complete only when we can integrate these two seemingly contradictory views. Similarly, in school algebra, the literal symbol x is at one and the same time both particular unknown and variable quantity. In taking a relationship-between-quantities or functions-based approach, one chooses to make the second, variable view of x central and the first, particular unknown view of x background, while traditionally the roles of these views are reversed. (pp. 77–78)

As Chazan points out, the view of variable as *unknown* has traditionally been the dominant view of variable in school algebra. Yet, the idea of variable as *changing quantity* is potentially very powerful as a tool for understanding relationships in mathematical and real-world situations. Reflect 1.12 invites you to explore these dual views of variable further.

stop reflect ➔
See Reflect 1.12 on p. 29.

→ → →

Two variables in this situation are *time* and *distance*. We think about one of these variables—distance—as an unknown when we ask a question like, "What distance will Cassie have run after 5 minutes?" This question asks us to find a particular number that is currently unknown—the distance that Cassie will have run after 5 minutes. In response, we can write an expression for the distance that Cassie will have run since starting the race as $186.7 \cdot t$, where t is the time in minutes (11.2 km/hr • 1 hr/60 min • 1000 m/1 km is 186.7 m/min). We can evaluate the expression $186.7 \cdot t$ to determine that Cassie will have run approximately 933.5 meters after 5 minutes:

$$186.7 \cdot t$$
$$186.7 \text{ m/min} \cdot 5 \text{ min}$$
$$933.5 \text{ m}$$

Reflect 1.12

Returning to the context of the service club's fundraisers, consider the following situation: Suppose that Cassie and Winston are student members of the service club and are planning to participate in the 5K run. Cassie runs at a constant rate of 11.2 kilometers per hour (186.7 meters per minute), and Winston runs at a constant rate of 13.7 kilometers per hour (228.3 meters per minute).

a. What are some of the variables in this situation?

b. What would it mean to think about the variables in this situation as *unknowns?* Write down some questions that you might ask about this situation that emphasize a view of *variables as unknowns.*

c. What would it mean to think about the variables in this situation as *changing quantities?* Write down some questions that you might ask about this situation that emphasize a view of *variables as changing quantities.*

d. What are some differences in the kind of information that you obtain when you think of *variables as unknowns* as compared with *variables as changing quantities?*

This information provides a "snapshot" of Cassie at one instant: At a time of 5 minutes, Cassie will be 933.5 meters into the race. By viewing the distance as a variable representing an unknown value, we gain information about particular positions along the run at particular times—"snapshots" of the situation.

By contrast, if we view the variable t simply as time elapsed since Cassie and Winston started the race without assigning any particular, known value to t, such as 5 minutes, we obtain some different information about the situation. When we view t as a changing quantity, the expression $186.7 \cdot t$ describes how Cassie's distance from the starting line varies as time passes once she starts the race. If we think about both distance and time as changing quantities, we might ask a question like, "As t increases from 0 to 5 minutes, how does Cassie's distance from the starting line change?" This question is, at first glance, only subtly different from the question posed in the previous paragraph. An important difference, however, is that the latter question focuses our attention on a relationship between two changing quantities—namely, distance run as a *function* of elapsed time. From this perspective, we can view the expression $186.7 \cdot t$ less as an expression for determining a single unknown value of t and more as a rule for a function. Emphasizing a view of variables as changing quantities is part of what is often referred to as a *functions-based approach* to algebra (Chazan 2000; Chazan and Yerulshalmy 2003; Fey et al. 1995; Heid 1996; Schwartz and Yerushalmy 1992).

Equality and Equivalence: Big Idea 3

Big Idea 3. *The equals sign indicates that two expressions are equivalent. It can also be used in defining or naming a single expression or function rule.*

In our exploration of Big Idea 3, which focuses on equality and solving equations, we will discuss two uses of the equals sign: to indicate that two expressions are equivalent and to give a name to a function rule. We will also explore solving equations and inequalities as well as the meaning of solutions to equations and inequalities.

Indicating *equivalence*

Essential Understanding 3a. *The equals sign can indicate that two expressions are equivalent.*

In our discussion of Big Idea 1, we determined that the expression $10x - 4x$ and the expression $6x$ are equivalent. We can write $10x - 4x = 6x$ to indicate that these two expressions are equivalent for all values of the variable x. When we use an equals sign to indicate that two expressions are equivalent, we have written an *equation.* Note that an equals sign can be used in a statement of equivalence of mathematical entities other than two expressions, although such use is not common in middle school mathematics. For example, we can use an equals sign to indicate that two functions or two matrices are equivalent.

Big Idea 1

Expressions are foundational for algebra; they serve as building blocks for work with equations and functions.

It is important to recognize that the equals sign is not a signal to perform a given computation (as the = button on some calculators might indicate), nor is it a signal that the answer to a problem comes next (as in = 6). These views of the equals sign represent very common misunderstandings, which Reflect 1.13 explores.

Reflect 1.13

If you were to show your students the following and ask them to figure out what number should replace "?", what answers do you think your students might give?

$$3 + 4 = ? + 2$$

Given the problem in Reflect 1.13, some students are likely to say that the number 7 should replace the question mark. Many researchers (e.g., Knuth et al. 2006) refer to this misunderstanding as an *operational view* of the equals sign; if we type "3 + 4 =" in some calculators, the immediate result is 7. An operational view is common among middle-grades students. Particularly troubling is the finding that such a view of the equals sign is associated with lower performance on equation-solving items (Knuth et al. 2006). In other words, students with an operational view of the equals sign not only fail to understand the concept of the equals sign but also perform relatively poorly when asked to solve equations.

Defining or naming an expression or function rule

Essential Understanding 3*b*. *The equals sign can be used in defining or giving a name to an expression or function rule.*

Another use of the equals sign is to give a name to an expression so that we can explore and represent it more easily. For example, if $30a$ is the cost in cents of purchasing a apples at 30 cents each, we may choose to use an equals sign to write $y = 30a$. The statement $y = 30a$ allows us to use the variable y instead of the expression $30a$ as we explore and represent this situation. We can also use function notation to make this assignment; we might write $f(a) = 30a$.

Understanding the difference between these two uses of the equals sign—as a way to indicate that two expressions are equivalent or as a way to name an expression—is fundamental to the study of algebra in two important ways. First, this distinction is related to the two different conceptions of variable that we described earlier. When we use the equals sign to indicate that two expressions are equivalent, we might be using variables as unknowns. As we will describe in more detail in a later example, the equation $10x + 20 = 5x + 50$ indicates that the expression $10x + 20$ and the expression $5x + 50$ are equivalent. In this equation, the variable x is an unknown quantity (Essential Understanding 2*b*), and we might be interested in knowing for what value(s) of the unknown these two expressions have the same value. By contrast, when we define a function (see the discussion of Big Idea 4) by using "=" with the function notation $f(x)$, as in $f(x) = 10x + 20$, we are using x to indicate a varying quantity (Essential Understanding 2*c*).

These two uses of the equals sign also relate to differences between a function and an equation. Reflect 1.14 invites consideration of the differences between these two important ideas in algebra.

Essential Understanding 2*b*
Using variables permits writing expressions whose values are not known or vary under different circumstances.

Big Idea 4

Functions provide a means for describing and understanding relationships between variables. They can have multiple representations—in algebraic symbols, situations, graphs, verbal descriptions, tables, and so on—and they can be classified into different families with similar patterns of change.

Essential Understanding 2*c*
Using variables permits representing varying quantities. This use of variables is particularly important in studying relationships between varying quantities.

Reflect 1.14

If one of your students asked you to explain the difference between a function and an equation, how would you respond?

Big Idea 4

Functions provide a means for describing and understanding relationships between variables. They can have multiple representations—in algebraic symbols, situations, graphs, verbal descriptions, tables, and so on—and they can be classified into different families with similar patterns of change.

For examples of functions that cannot be described by algebraic expressions, see *Developing Essential Understanding of Functions for Teaching Mathematics in Grades 9–12* (Cooney, Beckmann, and Lloyd 2010).

The distinction between functions and equations is somewhat subtle. After all, functions and equations, and the ways in which we represent them, appear to have many common features, such as equals signs, expressions, and variables. Furthermore, in many current middle school algebra textbooks, this distinction is not clearly addressed. Some textbooks focus primarily on equations, with only a brief mention of functions and little attempt to connect functions with equations. Other middle school textbooks focus almost exclusively on functions, with little or no attention to working with equations. More generally, some researchers have lamented the artificial separation of *function-oriented* views of algebra and *equation-oriented* views of algebra (Star and Rittle-Johnson 2009), including the suggestion that students' difficulties with algebra emerge at least in part from this disconnection.

Whereas an equation states that two expressions are equivalent for certain values of the variables, a function describes a relationship between varying quantities. Some functional relationships, but not all, can be described by an algebraic expression. For example, the function $f(x) = 10x + 20$ describes a relationship for which each input x has exactly one output $10x + 20$. For the input 2, the function has one output, $f(2)$, which can by obtained by computing $10 \cdot 2 + 20$. The use of functions allows us to explore a wide variety of expressions (e.g., linear and nonlinear), where each expression communicates information about how variables vary and how we can associate output values with given input values.

Equations become very useful in investigating relationships between two expressions. We explore ways that equations can be used to understand relationships between two expressions next. In our discussion of Big Idea 4, we will return to functions as a way to explore relationships between varying quantities that can be described by a single expression.

Finding the value(s) to make two expressions equivalent

Essential Understanding 3c. *It is often important to find the value(s) of a variable for which two expressions represent the same quantity.*

Essential Understanding 3*a* *The equals sign can indicate that two expressions are equivalent.*

One use of the equals sign is to indicate that two expressions are equivalent (Essential Understanding 3*a*). This use leads us to consider ways in which we might determine a value (if any such exists) or multiple values (if more than one exists) that we can substitute each time that a particular variable occurs in two expressions to produce expressions that are equivalent. In expressions that have more than one variable, the use of the equals sign leads us to consider ways of determining such values for each variable. Determining these values is something that we are often interested in doing, as Essential Understanding 3*c* suggests.

To explore ways of solving equations, consider again our student service club. This time, suppose that some of the students in the club are interested in joining a national service club. Although membership in the local school club is free, the two national service clubs that the students are thinking about joining, Kids Help and United Service, have membership fees. Kids Help has a one-time enrollment fee of $20 and a $10 per month membership fee. United Service has a one-time enrollment fee of $50 and a $5 per month membership fee. Some of the students think it is a better deal to join Kids Help because the one-time enrollment fee is lower. Others find the United Service membership more appealing because of the lower monthly rate. Still others claim that one club starts off as a better deal, but after a certain number of months, the other club becomes a better deal.

Let's consider possible ways to investigate the situation. We can use equations, tables, and graphs to help analyze these membership programs. We can represent the cost of membership in Kids Help after x months with the expression $10x + 20$, and the cost of membership in United Service with the expression $5x + 50$. As the table in figure 1.13 shows, the quantities that $10x + 20$ and $5x + 50$ represent are different for many values of x. Yet, finding the value at which the expressions are the same can help in understanding under what conditions one membership might be a better value than another. How, then, can we find the value of x (if such a value exists) for which $10x + 20$ and $5x + 50$ have the same value? The symbolic way of posing this question is to write $10x + 20 = 5x + 50$. This equation indicates our interest in finding the value(s) of x (if any exist) that make $10x + 20$ and $5x + 50$ have the same value. Such values can be found in many different ways, including making a table of values and graphing each expression.

For example, we might make a table like the one in figure 1.13, exploring the values of the expressions $10x + 20$ and $5x + 50$ for various values of the unknown variable x. As indicated in this table, when the value of the variable x is 6, the expressions $10x + 20$ and $5x + 50$ have the same value of 80. This means that, for memberships lasting exactly 6 months, students who joined Kids Help will have spent the same amount of money on membership as students who joined United Service.

Although tables are powerful and intuitive tools for exploring expressions, a table makes it difficult to rule out the possibility that there are other values for which the expressions are equal (consider Essential Understanding 4*d*). In this example, is there another value of x for which $10x + 20$ and $5x + 50$ have the same value? How many values of x would we need to list in our table before we were certain that there are not other such values?

Essential Understanding 4*d*
Some representations of a function may be more useful than others, depending on how they are used.

Months (x)	Cost of Kids Help membership ($10x + 20$)	Cost of United Service membership ($5x + 50$)
0	10(0) + 20, or 20	5(0) + 50, or 50
1	10(1) + 20, or 30	5(1) + 50, or 55
2	10(2) + 20, or 40	5(2) + 50, or 60
3	10(3) + 20, or 50	5(3) + 50, or 65
4	10(4) + 20, or 60	5(4) + 50, or 70
5	10(5) + 20, or 70	5(5) + 50, or 75
6	10(6) + 20, or 80	5(6) + 50, or 80
7	10(7) + 20, or 90	5(7) + 50, or 85
8	10(8) + 20, or 100	5(8) + 50, or 90

Fig. 1.13. A table showing the cost of membership in two service clubs after *x* months

We can also explore this same issue in graphs and perhaps avoid this limitation of a table. For the equation $10x + 20 = 5x + 50$, let's use $f(x)$ for the expression $10x + 20$ and $g(x)$ for the expression $5x + 50$. If we graph the function $f(x) = 10x + 20$ and the function $g(x) = 5x + 50$ on the same set of axes, we can look for the value(s)

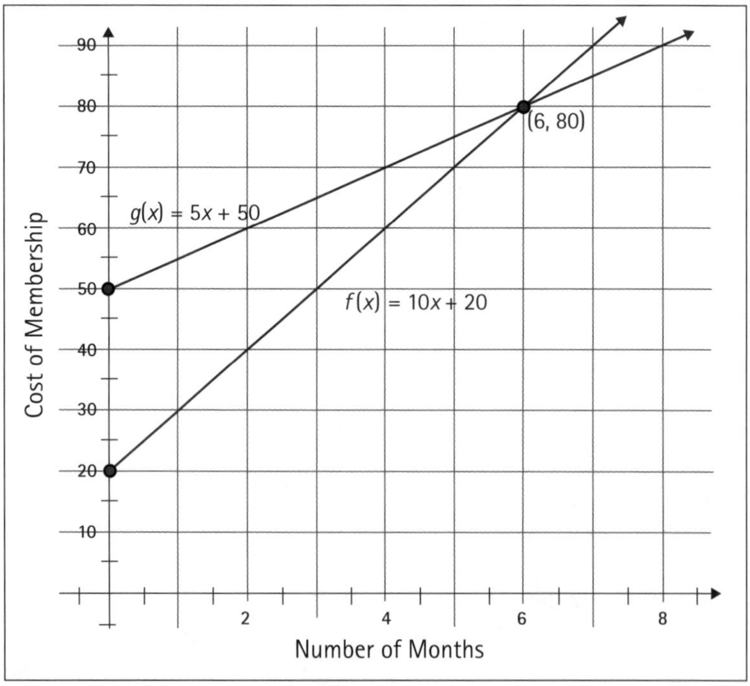

Fig. 1.14. The graphs of $f(x) = 10x + 20$ and $g(x) = 5x + 50$ intersect at the point (6, 80), showing that the cost of membership in two service clubs is the same ($80) if students belong for 6 months.

of x for which these two expressions have the same value. We can see in figure 1.14 that the two graphs intersect when x is 6, at the point (6, 80). This shows that the two memberships cost the same amount if the students belong to the clubs for six months.

Solving an equation

Essential Understanding 3*d*. *Finding the value(s) of a variable for which two expressions represent the same quantity is known as* solving an equation.

To solve an equation, we can apply a series of symbolic transformations to the equation so that in one expression we are left with only the variable, all by itself, and in the other expression we have only a number or numerical computation. If we are able to transform the equation in such a way that one expression consists only of the variable (e.g., $x =$) and the other is a number or numerical computation, then this process yields the value or values of the variable that make both expressions equivalent.

Essential Understanding 1c *A relatively small number of symbolic transformations can be applied to expressions to yield equivalent expressions.*

In our discussion of Essential Understanding 1*c*, we explored symbolic transformations that change the form of an expression without changing the quantity that it represents. Solving an equation requires us to consider symbolic transformations that we can make to the expressions on both sides of the equals sign without changing their equivalence. For example, consider the equation $2x = 6$. This equation indicates that we are interested in the value or values of the variable x for which the expression $2x$ has the same value as the expression 6. One way to solve this equation would be to multiply both expressions by $1/2$. This results in the equation $x = 3$. Because we have transformed one expression so that the variable is by itself on one side of the equals sign, we know that the other expression indicates the value of x for which the two expressions are equivalent (3). We can confirm this by finding the value of $2x$ when x is 3; $2 \cdot 3$ is 6. This transformation, multiplying both expressions in an equation by the same value, is one of several that we can use in solving equations. Multiplying both expressions by a constant (or dividing both by a nonzero constant) maintains the equality of two expressions because of the *multiplication property of equality*.

Similarly, the *addition property of equality* holds that the same value can be added to both expressions in an equation without changing the equivalence of the two expressions. Given the equation $x + 3 = 4$ (which states that the expression $x + 3$ and the expression 4 are equivalent for a particular value or values of the variable x), we can add -3 to both expressions to yield $x = 1$. This indicates that when x has value 1, the two expressions have the same value.

For more complex equations, it may be necessary to apply a series of symbolic transformations to solve the equation, including some of the symbolic transformations discussed previously for transforming expressions. Reflect 1.15 invites you to consider what kinds of symbolic transformations you might apply (and in what order) to solve a linear equation.

Reflect 1.15

How might you approach solving an equation like $10x + 20 = 5x + 50$? What steps would you be likely to take? Think about each step and justify why taking it makes sense.

Consider the equation $10x + 20 = 5x + 50$. As shown below, if we add the value -20 to both expressions, then add the value $-5x$ to both expressions (both of which ensure the equivalence of the two expressions by the addition property of equality), and finally multiply both expressions by $1/5$ (which ensures the equivalence of the expressions by the multiplication property of equality), we are left with $x = 6$:

$$\begin{aligned} 10x+20 &= 5x+50 \\ 10x+20+(-20) &= 5x+50+(-20) \\ 10x &= 5x+30 \\ 10x+(-5x) &= 5x+(-5x)+30 \\ 5x &= 30 \\ 5x\cdot\frac{1}{5} &= 30\cdot\frac{1}{5} \\ x &= 6 \end{aligned}$$

Examining these symbolic transformations *graphically* is a very useful way of illustrating that the transformations do not change the value(s) for which the two expressions are equivalent. Consider again the equation $10x + 20 = 5x + 50$ and the graph in figure 1.14 showing $f(x) = 10x + 20$ and $g(x) = 5x + 50$. Recall that the graphs of these two functions intersect at the point (6, 80). When we add (−20) to both expressions, we are left with $f_1(x) = 10x$ and $g_1(x) = 5x + 30$. Despite the fact that $f(x)$ and $f_1(x)$ are not equivalent, the x-value where $f_1(x) = g_1(x)$ is the same as the x-value where $f(x) = g(x)$. This can be seen in the graph in figure 1.15. The x-coordinate of the point of intersection is 6. As shown in figure 1.15, the graphs corresponding to f and g have been shifted down 20 units, so the intersection of the graphs of f_1 and g_1 is at (6, 60).

Similarly, when we add $(-5x)$ to both expressions, we are left with $f_2(x) = 5x$ and $g_2(x) = 30$. As before, we have transformed each expression in the same way, so the value of x for which $f_2(x) = g_2(x)$ is the same as in our previous equations, $f(x) = g(x)$ and $f_1(x) = g_1(x)$.

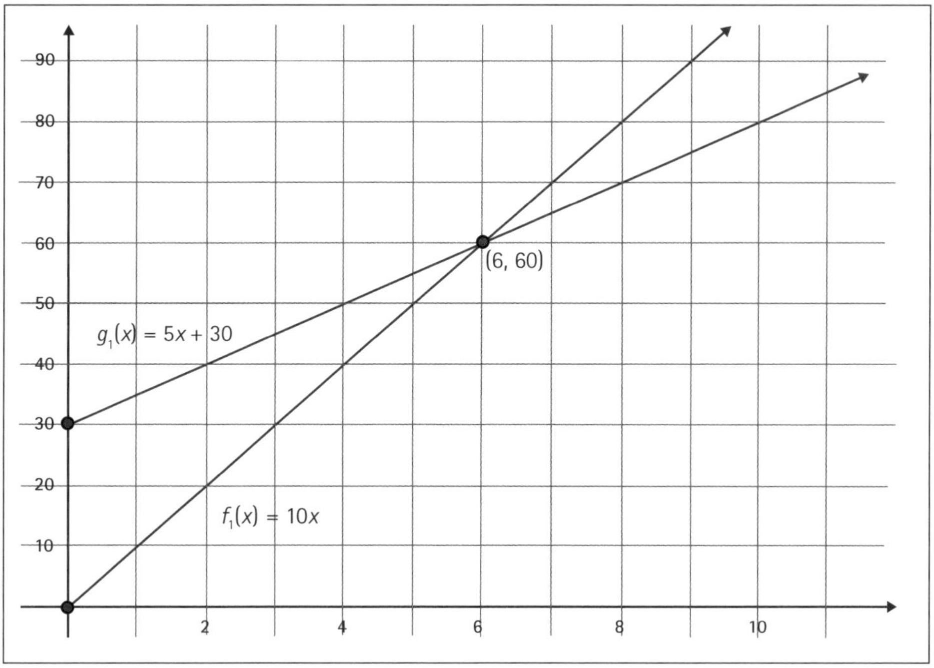

Fig. 1.15. The graphs of $f_1(x) = 10x$ and $g_1(x) = 5x + 30$ intersect at the point (6, 60).

This is illustrated in the graph of figure 1.16. Finally, when we multiply both expressions by $1/5$, we obtain $f_3(x) = x$ and $g_3(x) = 6$, which is shown graphically in figure 1.17.

We have examined graphically the pairs of functions involved at each step of the equation-solving process. Because we transformed the functions in each pair in the same way, the x-coordinates of the intersections of the graphs of the functions are the same ($x = 6$). We will return to this discussion of the relationship between symbolic

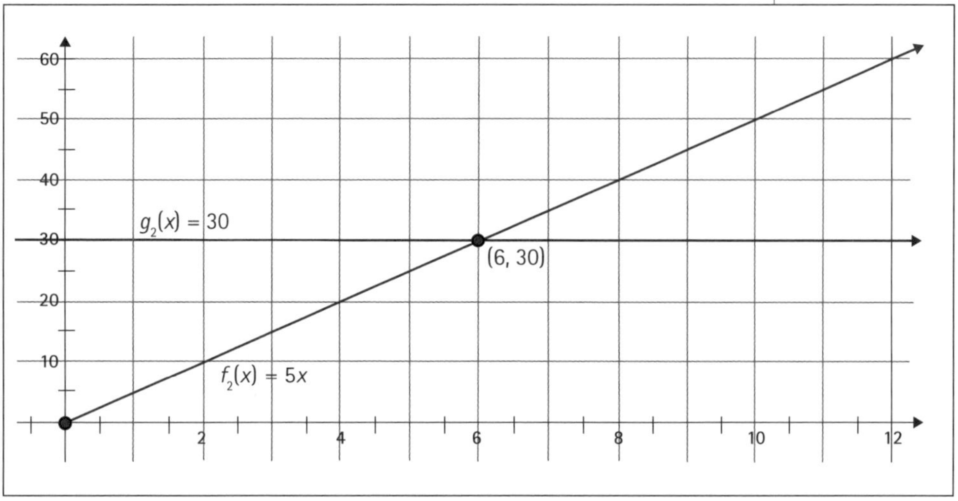

Fig. 1.16. The graphs of $f_2(x) = 5x$ and $g_2(x) = 30$ intersect at the point (6, 30).

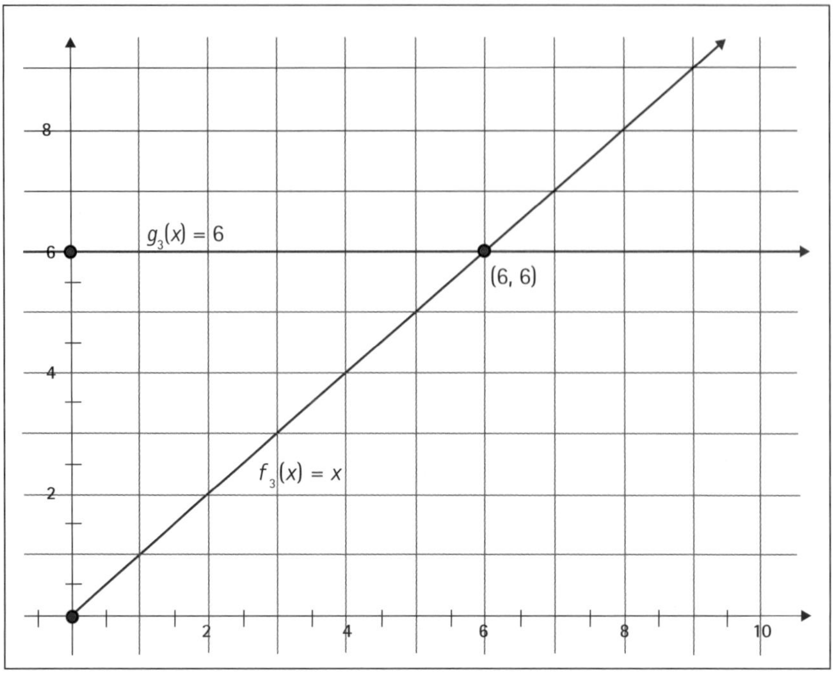

Fig. 1.17. The graphs of $f_3(x) = x$ and $g_3(x) = 6$ intersect at the point (6, 6).

and graphical transformations of functions later, as a way of developing a deeper understanding of families of functions, in our discussion of Big Idea 4.

Indicating a relationship other than equality

Essential Understanding 3e. *An inequality is another way to describe a relationship between expressions; instead of showing that the values of two expressions are equal, inequalities indicate that the value of one expression is greater than (or greater than or equal to) the value of the other expression.*

Big Idea 4

Functions provide a means for describing and understanding relationships between variables. They can have multiple representations—in algebraic symbols, situations, graphs, verbal descriptions, tables, and so on—and they can be classified into different families *with similar patterns of change.*

Inequalities are treated in very much the same way as equations. Whereas an equation presents us with an equals sign that indicates the equivalence of two expressions, an inequality has an inequality symbol that provides us with information about the relationship between the values of the two expressions. In particular, it tells us that one expression is greater than (or greater than or equal to) the other.

As we saw in the case of equations, graphical representations can be useful for illustrating inequalities. Consider an inequality in one variable, such as $x < 3$. This inequality indicates a relationship between the expression x and the expression 3, and the relationship is that x is less than 3. Because the inequality has only one variable, it can be shown on a single axis. The number line graph in figure 1.18 shows the values of x that make this relationship true.

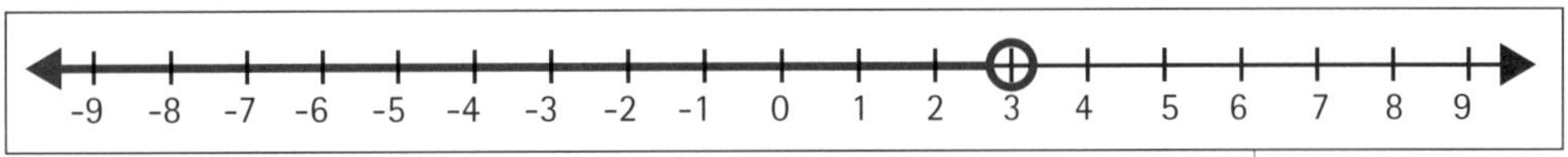

Fig. 1.18. A number line graph illustrating the inequality $x < 3$

In a number line graph of an inequality, it is customary to shade portions of the number line that represent all values of the variable(s) for which the indicated relationship between the two expressions holds. In the case of $x < 3$, the shaded portion of the number line represents all the numbers less than 3. For example, the point for number 1 is part of the shaded portion, since when x is 1, the inequality is $1 < 3$, which states a true relationship. On the other hand, the point for number 6 is not part of the shaded portion, because when x is 6, the inequality would be $6 < 3$, which is not true.

Solving inequalities

Essential Understanding 3f. *In solving an inequality, multiplying or dividing both expressions by a negative number reverses the sign* ($<$, $>$, $\leq$, $\geq$) *that indicates the relationship between the two expressions.*

Solving an inequality is very similar to solving an equation, in that we try to find the value(s) of the variables for which the indicated relationship between the expressions is true. In solving equations, we apply the addition property of equality when we add (or subtract) the same value on both sides of the equals sign and produce a new pair of equivalent expressions. Working in a parallel way, we can add the same value to, or subtract the same value from, both expressions in an inequality and preserve the particular relationship of inequality between the expressions. In this work, we are applying the *addition property of inequality.*

Let's revisit the example discussed previously, involving the students who are deciding which of two national service clubs, Kids Help and United Service, to join. Suppose that the students ask the question, "For what periods of time is membership in Kids Help less expensive than membership in United Service?" This question would be important to a student who wants to be a member for only a few months or to a student who plans to be a member for several years. Recall that Kids Help has a one-time enrollment fee of \$20 and a \$10 per month membership fee, and United Service has a one-time enrollment fee of \$50 and a \$5 per month membership fee.

Solving the inequality $10x + 20 < 5x + 50$ allows us to find the values for x for which membership in Kids Help is less expensive than membership in United Service. We can solve this inequality by a process that is similar to the process that we used to solve the equation $10x + 20 = 5x + 50$:

$$10x + 20 < 5x + 50$$
$$10x + 20 + (-20) < 5x + 50 + (-20)$$
$$10x < 5x + 30$$
$$10x + (-5x) < 5x + (-5x) + 30$$
$$5x < 30$$
$$5x \cdot \frac{1}{5} < 30 \cdot \frac{1}{5}$$
$$x < 6$$

What does this solution, $x < 6$, mean in the context of the cost comparison of the service club memberships? We see that for memberships that last less than 6 months, it makes financial sense to join Kids Help. For example, a 5-month membership at Kids Help costs $70, because 10(5) + 20 is 70. In contrast, a 5-month membership at United Service costs $75, because 5(5) + 50 is 75. However, for memberships longer than 6 months, United Service is a better deal. For example, a 7-month membership at Kids Help costs $90, because 10(7) + 20 is 90; in contrast, a 7-month membership at United Service costs $85, since 5(7) + 50 is 85.

Applying symbolic transformations to solve inequalities is different in one important way from applying them to solve equations. When we multiply or divide both expressions by a negative number, we must reverse the inequality sign to produce an equivalent inequality. Reflect 1.16 invites you to think about this difference between solving equations and solving inequalities.

Reflect 1.16

When multiplying or dividing both expressions in an inequality by a negative number, why do we reverse the inequality sign?

When multiplying or dividing both expressions by a negative number, we need to reverse the inequality sign in order to produce an equivalent inequality. Why is this the case? Let's first consider a numerical example, and then we will use graphs to explore why we reverse the inequality sign.

Consider the inequality 5 < 6, which indicates that 5 is less than 6. Let's multiply both 5 and 6 by the same positive value—say, 3:

$$5 < 6$$
$$5 \cdot 3 < 6 \cdot 3$$
$$15 < 18$$

In this case, we end up with 15 < 18, a statement that is also true.

What happens, however, if we multiply both 5 and 6 in the inequality 5 < 6 by the same negative value—say, –3? We seemingly end up with $-15 < -18$, a statement that is not true; -15 is greater than -18. To preserve the relationship between the two expressions indicated by the inequality $5 < 6$, we need to reverse the inequality sign:

$$5 < 6$$
$$5 \cdot (-3) > 6 \cdot (-3)$$
$$-15 > -18$$

Let's explore what is going on here by thinking about what happens when we multiply or divide by -1. For any real numbers a and b, if $a < b$, then $a - b < 0$, by the addition property of inequality (adding $-b$, or subtracting b from both sides of the inequality). Applying the addition property again and subtracting a from both sides, we obtain $-b < -a$. We can rewrite this inequality as $-a > -b$. This shows symbolically that if $a < b$, then $-a > -b$.

Conceptually, it can be helpful to think about how multiplication or division of the expressions in an inequality by -1 changes the expressions in the inequality to their "opposites," or additive inverses. Consider the number line shown in figure 1.19. The inequality $3 < 8$ is represented on the number line because 3 appears to the left of 8 on the line. When we multiply the two expressions in the inequality $3 < 8$ by -1, we must consider the relationship between the opposites of 3 and 8: -3 and -8, which are shown on the number line in figure 1.20. Because the locations of the opposites on this number line correspond to a reflection across the origin of the locations of the original points on the number line in figure 1.19, it makes sense that we would reverse the inequality sign when multiplying by -1.

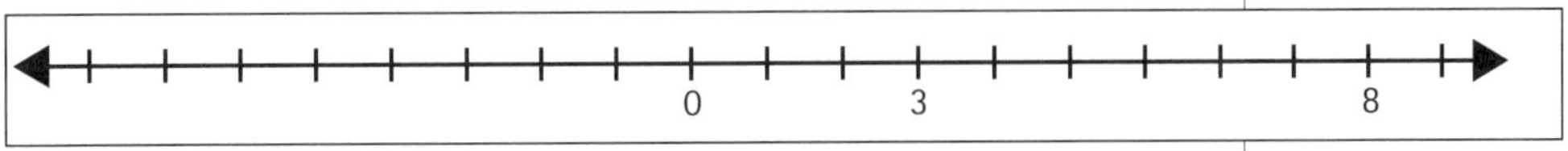

Fig. 1.19. A number line representing the inequality $3 < 8$

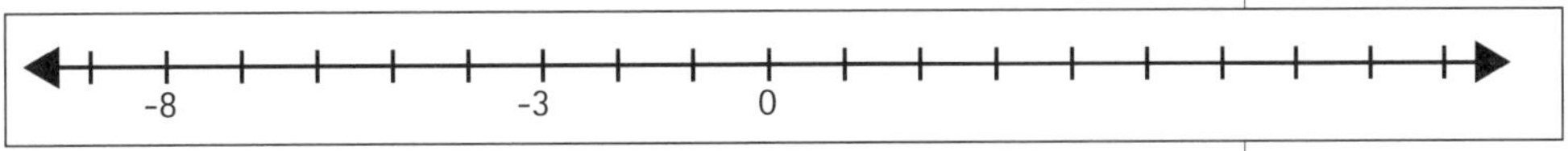

Fig. 1.20. A number line representing the inequality $-3 > -8$

What would happen if we had one positive and one negative number? Consider the inequality $-3 < 8$, shown in figure 1.21. When we multiply the expressions in the inequality by -1, we are considering the relationship between -8 and 3, the opposites of 8 and -3. We can see that $-8 < 3$ indicates a relationship that is true because -8 is to the left of 3 on the number line of figure 1.22. As in the previous example, when we multiply by -1, we reflect the number line across the origin, and we must reverse the inequality sign.

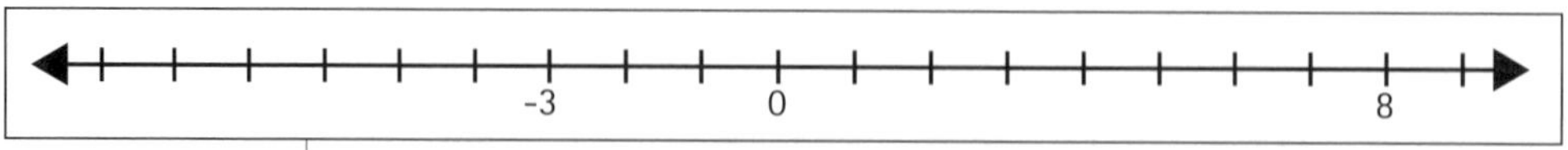

Fig. 1.21. A number line representing the inequality –3 < 8

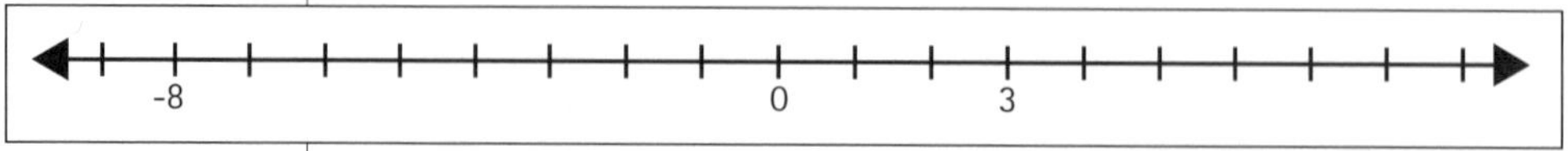

Fig, 1.22. A number line representing the inequality –8 < 3

You may wish to use number lines as we did in the examples above to explore on your own the case of an inequality with two negative numbers—for instance, $-8 < -3$. In general, multiplication or division by a negative number produces two expressions whose relationship to each other is the opposite of the original relationship between the two expressions, requiring us to reverse the inequality symbol to continue to have an inequality that is true. With these ideas in mind, consider Reflect 1.17.

Reflect 1.17

Think about what typically happens in the classroom when students are faced with solving an inequality such as $-3x \leq 12$. After dividing both sides of the inequality by –3, some students are likely to suggest that the solution to this inequality is $x \leq -4$. Instead of merely stating the rule about reversing the inequality sign, what representations or ideas might you draw on to help students understand that $x \leq -4$ is not the correct solution?

Exploring the solution of the inequality $-3x \leq 12$ graphically might be one way to help students think more carefully about the need to reverse the inequality sign when they are multiplying or dividing by a negative number. In particular, consider figure 1.23 below, in which the functions $f(x) = -3x$ and $g(x) = 12$ are graphed on the same axes.

The graphs corresponding to $f(x)$ and $g(x)$ intersect at the point (–4, 12). Part of the line for $f(x) = -3x$ lies above, and part of it lies below, the line for $g(x) = 12$. The portion of the line for $f(x) = -3x$ that corresponds to $x < -4$ (gray in the figure) lies above the line for $g(x) = 12$. The portion of the line for $f(x) = -3x$ that corresponds to $x > -4$, (purple in the figure) lies below the line for $g(x) = 12$. Solving the inequality $-3x \leq 12$ requires us to find all values of x for which the value of $-3x$ is less than (or equal to) 12. It may not be immediately obvious whether the solution consists of those values indicated in gray or those indicated in purple in the graph.

If we select two test points on the line $f(x) = -3x$—one in the gray portion of the line and one in the purple portion—we can determine which point represents a value of x that makes the inequality

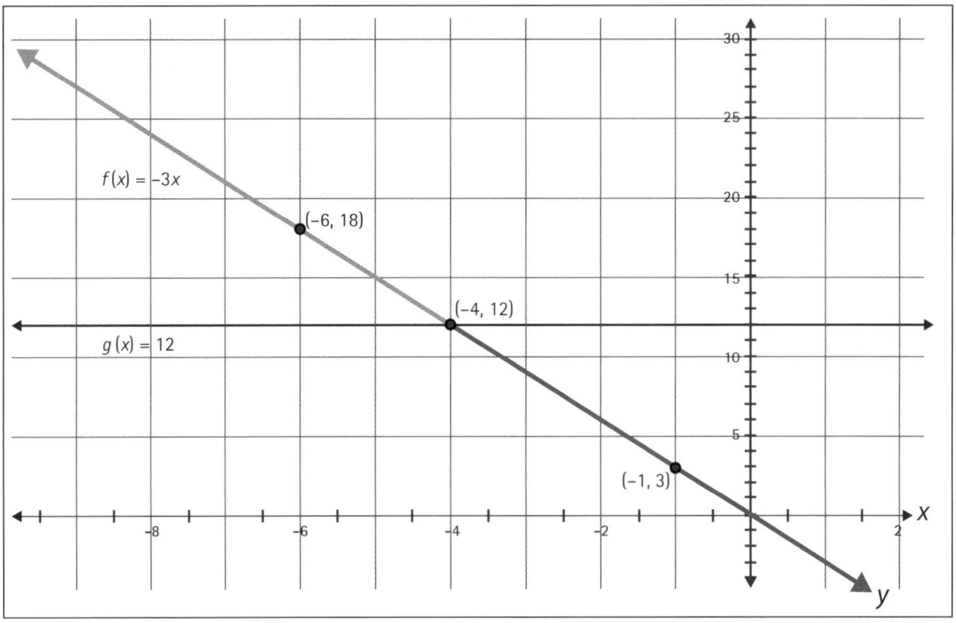

Fig. 1.23. Graphs of $f(x) = -3x$ and $g(x) = 12$ to aid in solving the inequality $-3x \le 12$

$-3x \le 12$ true. Consider the point (-6, 18) in the gray portion. Does its x-coordinate make the inequality true? Because -3(-6) is 18, and 18 is greater than 12, the x-coordinate of point (-6, 18) does not make the inequality $-3x \le 12$ a true statement. It follows that no gray points have x-coordinates that will make the inequality true. By contrast, consider the purple point (-1, 3). When $x = -1$, $f(x)$ is -3(-1), or 3, and 3 is less than 12, so the x-coordinate for point (-1, 3) does make the inequality $-3x \le 12$ true. This means that all purple points (in other words, where $x > -4$), in addition to the point where $x = -4$, correspond to solutions of the inequality. Thus, the solution to the inequality $-3x \le 12$ is given by $x \ge -4$.

This strategy—of graphically representing inequalities, picking a few points from key regions of the graph, and testing to see whether values corresponding to these points make the inequality true—is an extremely useful way to identify the correct solution set and avoid making the common error of forgetting to reverse the inequality sign when multiplying or dividing by a negative number. Moreover, by working with graphical solutions to inequalities, we reinforce the important idea that shaded points on the graph of an inequality are the ordered pairs that make the inequality true.

Another interesting approach to Reflect 1.17 might be to compare graphical representations of the equalities $-3x \le 12$ and $3x \ge -12$. In keeping with our earlier discussion of reflections of number lines, the graphical representation of $3x \ge -12$ is a reflection across the vertical axis of the graphical representation of the inequality $-3x \le 12$.

Representing and Analyzing Functions: Big Idea 4

Big Idea 4. *Functions provide a means for describing and understanding relationships between variables. They can have multiple representations—in algebraic symbols, situations, graphs, verbal descriptions, tables, and so on—and they can be classified into different families with similar patterns of change.*

Big Idea 3

The equals sign indicates that two expressions are equivalent. It can also be used in defining or naming a single expression or function rule.

In our discussion of Big Idea 3, we described a function as a relationship between varying quantities. In this section, we develop this idea further. A function is a relationship between an input (or *independent variable*) and an output (or *dependent variable*), with exactly one output for each input. The set of values for the input of a function is called its *domain*, and the set of all possible output values is its *range*. We can view a function f as an assignment of each input x from the domain to exactly one output $f(x)$ in the range.

Most functions that students encounter in grades 6–8 can be described by expressions and have domains that are subsets of the real numbers. For example, the function $f(x) = 5x - 3$ (which we often write as $y = 5x - 3$) is described by an algebraic expression and has the real numbers as its domain. We obtain an output for this function by multiplying an input by 5 and subtracting 3. The notation $f(x) = 5x - 3$ indicates that we can evaluate the function for values in the domain by substituting those values into the expression that defines the function. For instance, $f(10) = 5 \cdot 10 - 3$, so the value of $f(x)$ when $x = 10$ is 47.

Using functions to model how variables change together

Essential Understanding 4a. *Functions provide a tool for describing how variables change together. Using a function in this way is called* modeling, *and the function is called a* model.

Functions are very useful tools for describing how variables change together. In the function rule $f(x) = 5x - 3$, every unit increase in the input x corresponds to an increase of 5 in the output $f(x)$. For instance, $f(10) = 47$, and $f(11) = 52$. When we analyze the way in which one variable changes as the other changes, we can develop an understanding of the pattern of change of the function. As we will discuss in more detail later, different patterns of change provide a way for us to classify functions into families on the basis of the kinds of mathematical and real-world situations that they can model (Essential Understanding 4c). For example, linear functions are characterized by a constant additive increase or decrease; that is, for any unit increase in the input, the output increases (or decreases) by a constant amount. We will focus first on the pattern of change in linear relationships; later, we will discuss nonlinear relationships, including those described by quadratic and exponential functions.

Linearity in multiple representations

Essential Understanding 4b. *Functions can be represented in multiple ways—in algebraic symbols, situations, graphs, verbal descriptions, tables, and so on—and these representations, and the links among them, are useful in analyzing patterns of change.*

Equations, tables, and graphs are all representations that can assist us in understanding patterns and relationships between variables. Recall the situation in Reflect 1.12: Cassie and Winston, who plan to run in the 5K run organized by the service club, run at constant rates of 11.2 kilometers per hour (186.7 meters per minute) and 13.7 kilometers per hour (228.3 meters per minute), respectively. We looked at the expression $186.7 \cdot t$ to explore the relationship between distance and time in Cassie's case.

When we view such an expression as a function, we can use various representations to explore the situation that we are modeling. Graphing calculators and spreadsheets, as well as other technologies, can help us generate and explore tables and graphs efficiently, so that patterns in and between variables become more apparent. In particular, in the situation in Reflect 1.12, if we let d_1 represent the distance that Cassie has run after t minutes, we can write $d_1 = 186.7 \cdot t$ to describe the relationship between the distance d_1 and the number of minutes t that she has run. Similarly, we can write $d_2 = 228.3 \cdot t$ to describe the relationship between Winston's distance and the number of minutes that he has run. Consider Reflect 1.18, which suggests making tables to aid in probing the patterns of change of these two functions.

Essential Understanding 4c
One important way of describing functions is by identifying the rate at which the variables change together. It is useful to group functions into families with similar patterns of change because these functions, and the situations that they model, share certain general characteristics.

Reflect 1.18

Use a graphing calculator or spreadsheet to generate tables for the equations $d_1 = 186.7 \cdot t$ and $d_2 = 228.3 \cdot t$.

What important features of each of these relationships do you gain access to in the tables?

Describing functions by their rates of change

Essential Understanding 4c. *One important way of describing functions is by identifying the rate at which the variables change together. It is useful to group functions into families with similar patterns of change because these functions, and the situations that they model, share certain general characteristics.*

See *Developing Essential Understanding of Ratios, Proportions, and Proportional Reasoning for Teaching Mathematics in Grades 6–8* (Lobato and Ellis 2010) for additional discussion of rates and their relationship to ratios.

The idea of *rate* is central to the work that we do in analyzing functional situations. Describing the *rate of change* in a relationship—in other words, how one variable changes with respect to the other variable—can provide us with important information about a situation. Figure 1.24 shows a table that displays Cassie's and Winston's distances from the starting line at the end of each 1-minute interval for the first 9 minutes of the race. The values in the table indicate that for each 1-minute increase in time, Cassie's distance from the starting line increases by 186.7 meters and Winston's distance from the starting line increases by 228.3 meters.

Time since starting the race (min)	Cassie's distance from the starting line (m)	Winston's distance from the starting line (m)
0	0	0
1	186.7	228.3
2	373.4	456.6
3	560.1	684.9
4	746.8	913.2
5	933.5	1141.5
6	1120.2	1369.8
7	1306.9	1598.1
8	1493.6	1826.4
9	1680.3	2054.7

Fig. 1.24. A table representing Cassie's and Winston's distances over time

In both of these functions, the *change in distance* that relates to a particular *change in time* is the same over the course of the race. For example, over any 1-minute interval in the race, Cassie's distance will increase by 186.7 meters. This change is visible in successive entries in the second column in figure 1.24. As seen in the third column, over any 1-minute interval in the race, Winston's distance will increase by 228.3 meters. Similarly, over any 2-minute interval, Cassie's distance will increase by 373.4 meters (2 • 186.7), and Winston's distance will increase by 456.6 meters (2 • 228.3), regardless of the start of the interval of time.

In a linear relationship, the ratio of change in input to change in output is always the same, so we say that there is a *constant rate of change* between the variables (Essential Understanding 4e). Although Cassie's and Winston's distances from the starting line change at different rates, both rates of change are constant.

Essential Understanding 4e
Linear functions have constant rates of change.

Graphs of linear functions are lines. The graphs in figure 1.25 illustrate how the data for Cassie's and Winston's distances over time in the 5K race can be represented by segments of two lines. Because each unit of time corresponds to a constant increase in distance, the points on the graphs lie on a line.

The graphs in figure 1.25 make clear that Cassie will never catch up with Winston as long as they both keep running at their respective constant rates. In a graph of a linear function, the slope of the line represents the rate of change. A line's slope describes its steepness as well as its direction. In the case of Cassie's and Winston's distances over time, the slopes of both lines are positive because the functions are increasing. The slope of the gray line (modeling Winston's distance as a function of time) is greater than the slope of the purple line (modeling Cassie's distance as a function of time). Informally, we can say, "The gray line is steeper than the purple line."

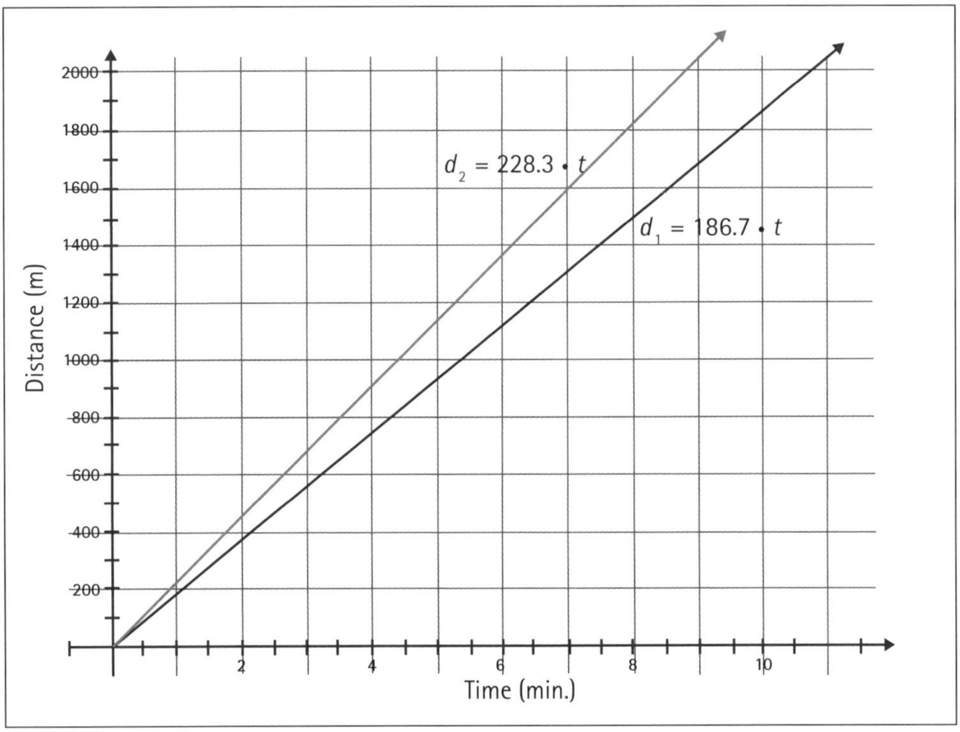

Fig. 1.25. Graphs representing Winston's (gray) and Cassie's (purple) distances over time

Different uses for different representations

Essential Understanding 4d. *Some representations of a function may be more useful than others, depending on how they are used.*

In our examination of the table in figure 1.24, we noticed that over any 1-minute interval in the race, Cassie's distance will increase by 186.7 m, regardless of the start of the time interval. The rate of change in the linear function d_1 is described by the ratio 186.7 meters to every 1 minute. This ratio is visible in the table, and it is also apparent in the graph: for any point on the purple line of the graph, if we move 1 unit to the right, we must also move up 186.7 units to stay on the line. Reflect 1.19 asks you to think about the slope of the graph for Winston's distance over time.

Reflect 1.19

What ratio is involved in the function that models Winston's distance over time? How is this ratio related to the function rule $d_2 = 228.3 \bullet t$?

In the case of Winston's distance over time, we were able to see in the table in figure 1.24 that over any 1-minute time interval, the distance increases by 228.3 meters. So, the function rule

$$d_2 = 228.3 \cdot t$$

describes a relationship in which the ratio of the change in distance to the corresponding change in time is always the same (228.3 m per min).

It is helpful to think about how the constant *rate of change* in a linear function appears in different representations of the function:

- In a table, the value of one variable increases or decreases by a constant amount as the value of the other variable increases by a constant amount.
- In a graph, the points lie on a line, and the constant rate of change is represented by the *slope*—the steepness and direction—of the line.
- The symbolic rule or expression for a linear function relating two variables x and y can be written in the form $y = mx + b$, where m is the constant rate of change and b is the value of y when $x = 0$.

We have begun to explore some of the unique characteristics of linear functions by considering several proportional relationships in the situation of the 5K race. Linear functions can model many real-world situations, including the following:

- The cost of buying x T-shirts at $4 per shirt (cost as a function of the number of items purchased)

- Income earned from pledges to dance x hours in a dance-a-thon (income as a function of the number of hours danced)
- The progress of a student running a 5K at a steady pace after x minutes (distance as a function of elapsed time)

What characteristics do these situations have in common? Consider Reflect 1.20 to explore this question.

Reflect 1.20

What characteristics do linear functions have in common? The situations that we have just identified relate to three fundraisers planned by the student service club: the T-shirt sale, the dance-a-thon, and the 5K race. What shared features allow these three situations to be modeled by linear functions?

Linear functions—constant rates of change

Essential Understanding 4e. *Linear functions have constant rates of change.*

To be modeled by a linear function, each of the situations in Reflect 1.20 must involve a rate that remains *constant*. In the T-shirt fundraiser, we have equally priced items (price per item is constant); in the dance-a-thon, we have a fixed hourly pledge (dollars earned per hour of dancing is constant); and in the 5K run, we have a steady running speed (distance run per unit of time is constant). Such constant rates of change are the focus of Essential Understanding 4*e*. Because rate of change is central to distinguishing among types of functions and identifying situations that can be modeled by different families of functions, it is important that we develop this idea further. To begin, consider the situation described in Reflect 1.21.

← ← ←

stop reflect

See Reflect 1.21 on p. 50.

Profit is a function of the number of T-shirts sold and is determined by the income from selling n T-shirts at \$15 apiece minus the club's expenditures for buying and silk-screening 100 T-shirts (\$500 + \$250). For each T-shirt sold, the profit increases by a constant amount: \$15. This constant rate of change in profit (\$15 for every shirt sold) can be seen in a table of values representing the situation, as shown in figure 1.26.

	+1 →	+1 →	+1 →	+1 →	+1 →	+1 →	
T-shirts sold (n)	0	1	2	3	4	5	6
Profit (P)	−750	−735	−720	−705	−690	−675	−660
	+15 →	+15 →	+15 →	+15 →	+15 →	+15 →	

Fig. 1.26. A table illustrating a constant rate of change in profit. For each shirt sold, the profit increases by \$15.

Reflect 1.21

Consider the following situation:

In preparing for their upcoming T-shirt sale, students in the service club purchased 100 T-shirts that cost $5 each and then spent $2.50 on each T-shirt for silk-screening. The club members then decided to charge customers $15 a T-shirt. The club is hoping to make a large profit from selling this set of 100 T-shirts.

Create a table and graph to help you answer the following questions:

a. Describe in words the relationship between profit and the number of T-shirts sold.

b. What patterns can you find in the way in which one quantity varies in relationship to another quantity?

c. Write a rule or expression for this relationship.

The constant rate of change in this situation can also be seen in a table with increments other than 1 in the values for 1 (for "T-shirts sold"). For example, in the table in figure 1.27, the number of T-shirts sold increases by 10. In this table, we can see that the profit increases by a constant amount of $150 for each increment of 10. In linear functions, the ratio of change in input to change in output is always the same; the ratio "$150 to 10 T-shirts sold" describes the rate of change. This ratio is equivalent to the ratio $15 to 1 T-shirt sold. Reflect 1.22 provides an opportunity to consider the rate of change further.

stop → reflect

See Reflect 1.22 on p. 51.

→ → →

Recall that *rate of change* refers to how one variable changes with respect to the other. In a linear function, the ratio of change in the input to the corresponding change in the output is constant. So we can consider differences between *any* pairs of corresponding values in the table. For example, a change in *n* from 20 to 60 corresponds to a change in *P* from –$450 to $150. This data gives rise to the ratio ($150 – (–$450)) to (60 – 20) T-shirts sold. Notice that this ratio, $600 to 40 T-shirts sold, is equivalent to $15 to 1 T-shirt sold.

	+10→	+10→	+10→	+10→	+10→	+10→	
T-shirts sold (*n*)	0	10	20	30	40	50	60
Profit (*P*)	–750	–600	–450	–300	–150	0	150
	+150→	+150→	+150→	+150→	+150→	+150→	

Fig. 1.27. A table illustrating a constant rate of change between *P* and *n*, with increments of 10 in *n*. For every 10 shirts sold, the profit increases by $150.

Reflect 1.22

When examining the tables in figures 1.26 and 1.27, we used differences between consecutive values for profit (P) and the number of T-shirts sold (n) to find the rate of change of $15 per T-shirt sold. To find the rate of change, is it necessary to consider differences between *consecutive* pairs of values in the table, or can we consider *any* two pairs of values?

The commonly used phrase "rise over run" refers to the ratio rise/run. This ratio is a way of describing the ratio of the *change in the output variable* to the corresponding *change in the input variable* of the function—in other words, the rate of change of the function. In the situation of the T-shirt sale, *rise* is the change in the profit (P), and *run* is the corresponding change in the number of T-shirts sold (n). *Rise* corresponds to vertical change in the graph (change in P), in contrast to *run*, which corresponds to horizontal change in the graph:

$$\frac{\text{rise}}{\text{run}} = \frac{\text{change in } P}{\text{change in } n}$$

Although slope is commonly described as "change," it is not that simple. The change in P has to be the change that corresponds to the change in n. For example, using the values in the table in figure 1.27, if the change in P used to form the ratio is based on the amount added to, say, 0 to yield 150 (+150), then the corresponding change in n is the amount added to 50 to get 60 (+10, not −10). If the change in P is the amount added to, say, 50 to get 30 (−20), then the corresponding change in n is the amount added to 0 to get −300.

Although we use the term "rise," the "rise" is negative when the line slopes downward (Cooney, Beckmann, and Lloyd 2010, p. 37), and we assume the run is positive. The ratio rise/run is the rate of change in the relationship and is the slope of the line when the relationship is represented graphically. It provides information about both the steepness and the direction of the line. It is important to recognize that for any linear function, all of the rise/run ratios are equivalent—an idea explored previously in Reflect 1.21.

Let's revisit the idea that all of the rise-to-run ratios are equivalent and constitute the rate of change of a linear function. A graph for the profit situation appears in figure 1.28. The points in the graph of this relationship lie on a line because increases in profit are constant with respect to the number of T-shirts sold. The profit increases steadily from its starting point of −$750 (when no T-shirts have been sold) to a positive amount (once more than 50 T-shirts have been sold).

What can we say about the rate of change by looking at the line? In figure 1.29, we zoom in on the graph to look at the line

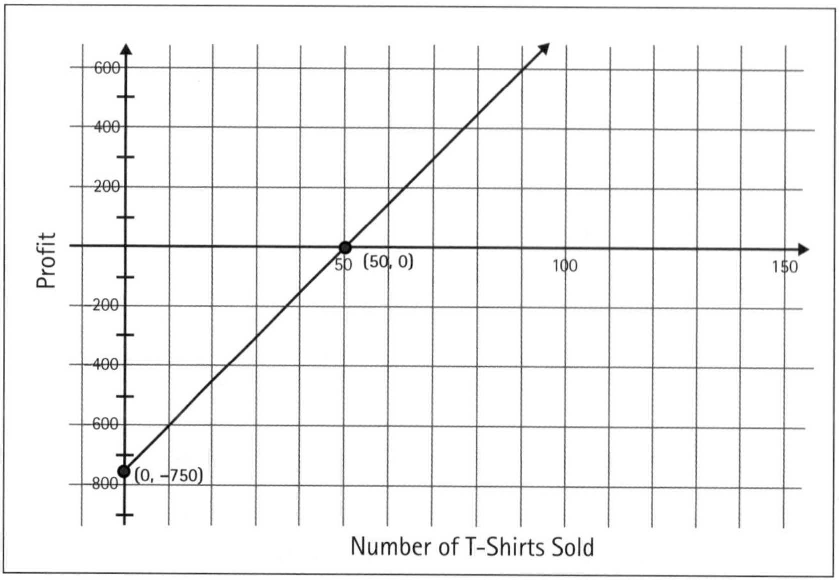

Fig. 1.28. Because the rate of change in the relationship between profit and number of shirts sold is constant, the points of the graph lie on a line.

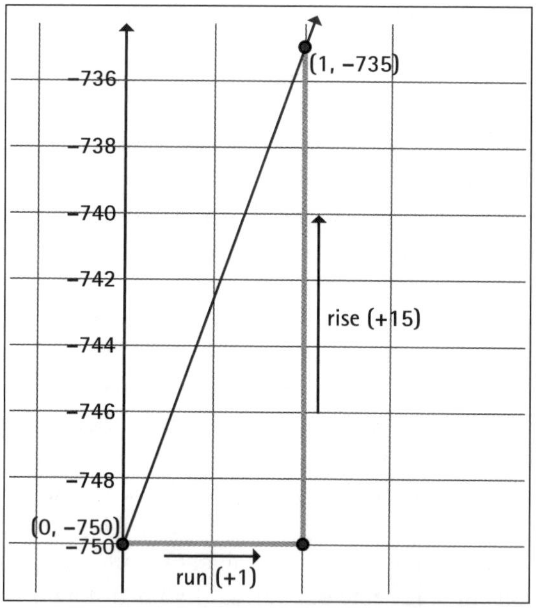

Fig. 1.29. A slope triangle representing the ratio of change in profit to change in number of shirts sold

between the points (0, –\$750) and (1, –\$735). Notice that we can form a triangle from a horizontal "run" segment (the difference between two x-values), a vertical "rise" segment (the difference between two y-values), and a segment of the line itself. This triangle is an example of a *slope triangle*. The slope triangle provides a graphical representation of the ratio rise/run, which is equivalent to ($15)/(1 T-shirt sold), or $15 per T-shirt sold.

The graph in figure 1.30 displays two other slope triangles. Note that the three rise/run ratios are equivalent: 300/20 = 150/10 = 15/1. Why do we obtain ratios equivalent to 15 to 1, regardless of which pairs of corresponding values we choose? We discussed this question earlier in relation to Reflect 1.22. Reflect 1.23 revisits this question, this time by using similar triangles.

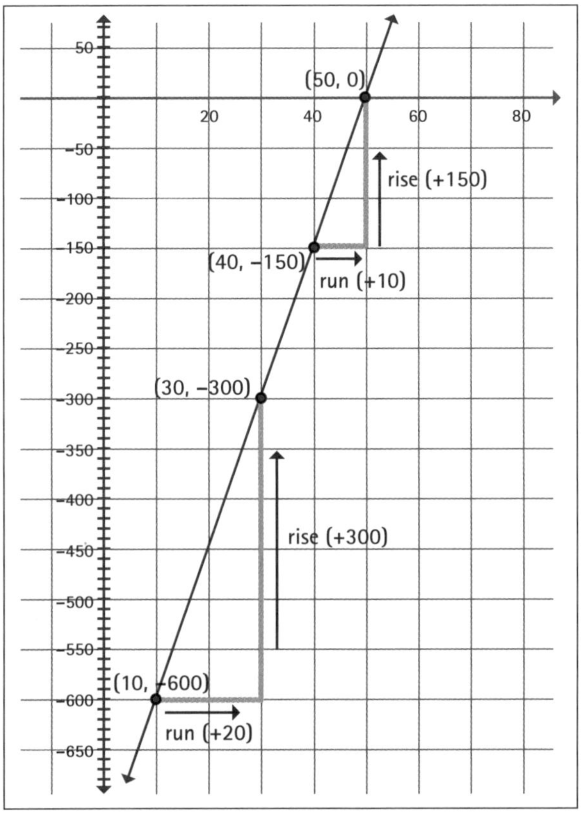

Fig. 1.30. More slope triangles with rise-to-run ratios equivalent to $15 of profit to 1 T-shirt sold

Reflect 1.23

Consider the two triangles in figure 1.30. These two triangles are *similar* to each other. (They are also similar to the slope triangle in figure 1.29, as well as to any other slope triangle for this line.) What does it mean for triangles to be similar, and why are these triangles similar?

Triangles are *similar* when their corresponding angles have the same measure. Equivalently, corresponding sides of similar triangles have lengths that are in the same ratio. The slope triangles are similar because their corresponding angles are congruent. (The horizontal

Additional discussion of slope and slope triangles appears in *Developing Essential Understanding of Functions for Teaching Mathematics in Grades 9–12* (Cooney, Beckmann, and Lloyd 2010).

sides of the triangles all form the same angle with the line, and the triangles are right triangles. So, all corresponding angles are congruent.) Because any slope triangles that we draw on the line will be similar, the corresponding sides have lengths in the same ratio—in other words, rise/run ratios will be equal. This idea of slope triangles provides a natural connection, again, to the idea of proportion. The ratio of any vertical change (rise) to its corresponding horizontal change (run) is constant in a linear relationship.

We have explored tabular and graphical representations of linear functions in detail. It can also be very useful to have a rule or expression that describes the relationship between the variables in a situation. In the situation of the T-shirt sale, we have seen that the rate of change in profit is \$15 for every T-shirt sold. For every T-shirt sold, the club takes in \$15. This idea can be represented by the expression $15n$. However, this expression does not take into account the \$750 in debt incurred in purchasing and silk-screening 100 T-shirts. So we need to include –750 in our function rule. The expression $15n - 750$ captures the profit for a given number of T-shirts sold. This function rule, $P = 15n - 750$, has the slope-intercept form of a linear function, $y = mx + b$, where m is the constant rate of change (or slope) and b is the value of y when $x = 0$ (the y-intercept; sometimes called the "starting point" in applied situations like that of the 5K race, where the smallest value is zero).

Understanding the role of m and b in linear expressions is an important part of using linear functions to model both real-world and purely mathematical relationships. Consider the tasks in Reflect 1.24.

Reflect 1.24

In the situation of the T-shirt sale, the function rule $P = 15n - 750$ describes the relationship between the profit, P, and the number of T-shirts sold, n.

a. Write a rule for a different relationship between P and n that has a graph with a steeper line than the graph in figure 1.28.

b. Write a rule for a different relationship between P and n that has a graph with a decreasing, rather than increasing, profit.

c. Write a rule for a different relationship between P and n that has a graph with a different y-intercept, or "starting point."

d. On a graphing calculator, create a graph to test each of the rules that you wrote, making sure to use a window that shows the graph clearly.

All rules in which the coefficient of n is greater than 15 correspond to graphs with steeper lines than the graph of $P = 15n - 750$. This makes sense because coefficients greater than 15 correspond to a line with a greater rise for every segment of run, creating a steeper angle with respect to the horizontal axis. When the slope is 15, each horizontal unit change (run) corresponds to a vertical change by 15 units (rise). When the slope is greater than 15, each horizontal unit change (run) corresponds to a vertical change by more than 15 units (rise). Thus, the line will be steeper than a line with a slope of 15. A function rule like $P = 200 - 100n$ has a graph that has a different vertical intercept, (0, 200), and is decreasing. Each unit increase in n corresponds to a decrease of 100 in P. This rule satisfies the requirements of parts (*b*) and (*c*) of Reflect 1.24.

Explorations of this sort are helpful because they focus attention on links between symbolic and graphical representations of linear functions. Reflect 1.25 offers another opportunity of this sort.

Reflect 1.25

Enter each set of equations below into a graphing calculator. What do you observe about each set of equations and their corresponding graphs?

Set 1	Set 2	Set 3
$y = .25x$	$y = -.5x$	$y = x - 3$
$y = .75x$	$y = -x$	$y = x - 1$
$y = x$	$y = -1.5x$	$y = x$
$y = 2x$	$y = -2x$	$y = x + 2$
$y = 2.5x$	$y = -3x$	$y = x + 3$

Graphs corresponding to the equations in set 1 have different slopes, all of which are positive. For graphs of equations in this set, slope triangles with a "run" of +1 will have positive "rises," as shown in figure 1.31. By contrast, the equations in set 2 correspond to graphs with negative slopes. These graphs are lines that slant downward instead of upward from left to right as x increases. The lines corresponding to the equations in set 3 have the same slope, so they are parallel to each other; however, the lines intersect the y-axis at different places (i.e., they have different y-intercepts). Understanding lines as functions from a holistic perspective, such as Reflect 1.26 calls for, allows us to consider lines as objects that act in particular ways.

Reflect 1.26

What geometric transformations of the graph of $y = x$, the equation corresponding to the simplest linear function, are involved in constructing graphs for each of the following linear equations?

$$y = 3x \qquad y = -0.5x$$

$$y = x - 2 \qquad y = -0.5x + 4$$

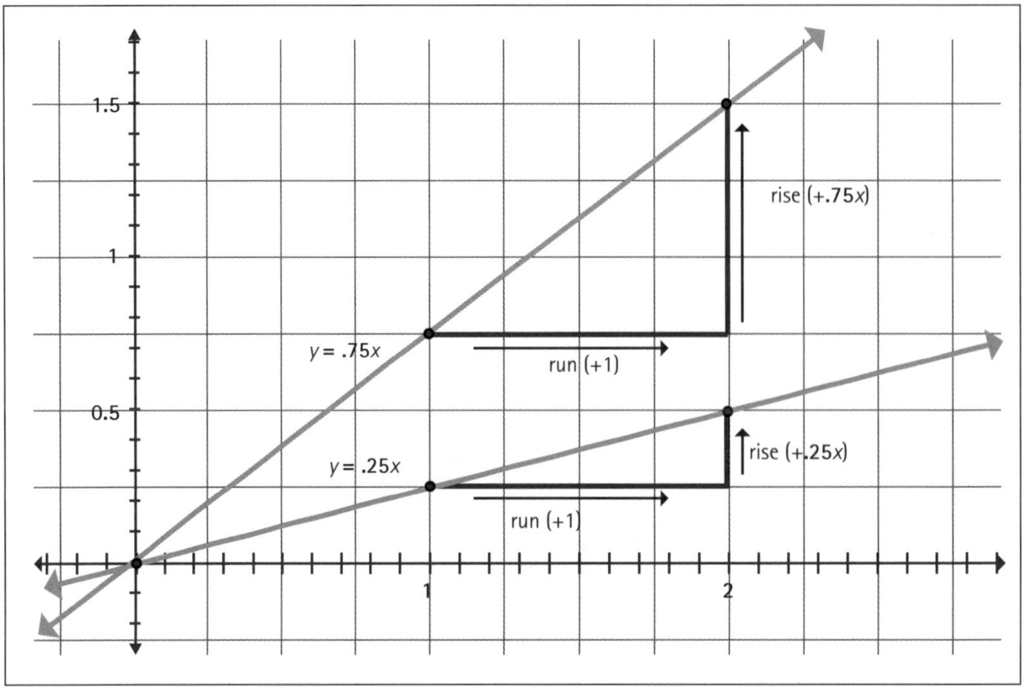

Fig. 1.31. Slope triangles for lines with differing slopes

An extended discussion of transformations appears in *Developing Essential Understanding of Geometry for Teaching Mathematics in Grade 6–8* (Sinclair, Pimm, and Skelin, forthcoming).

When exploring lines as objects, we can make another interesting connection—to transformational geometry. Reflect 1.26 invites you to look at connections between geometric transformations of lines on the coordinate plane and the different slopes and y-intercepts in symbolic representations of linear functions.

In figure 1.32, we can see that the graph of $y = x - 2$ is a vertical *translation* of the graph of $y = x$. To construct the graph of $y = x - 2$, we can simply shift the graph of $y = x$ down two units. We can also see that multiplication of x by a positive constant greater than 1, as in the case of $y = 3x$, results in a graph that is steeper than the graph of $y = x$.

When we multiply x by a negative constant, as in $y = -0.5x$, the result is a line that is *reflected* across the x-axis. The graph of $y = x$ increases as x increases, but the graph of $y = -0.5x$ decreases as x increases. Because $0 < 0.5 < 1$, the graph of $y = -0.5x$ is less steep than the graph of $y = x$. In other words, the graph of $y = -0.5x$ decreases as x increases less quickly than the graph of $y = x$ increases. (Recall figure 1.31 for an illustration with slope triangles of why this is the case.) The graph of $y = -0.5x + 4$ reflects the line for the graph of $y = x$ across the x-axis, reduces the steepness of the line, and shifts the resulting decreasing graph in the positive (upward) direction by four units.

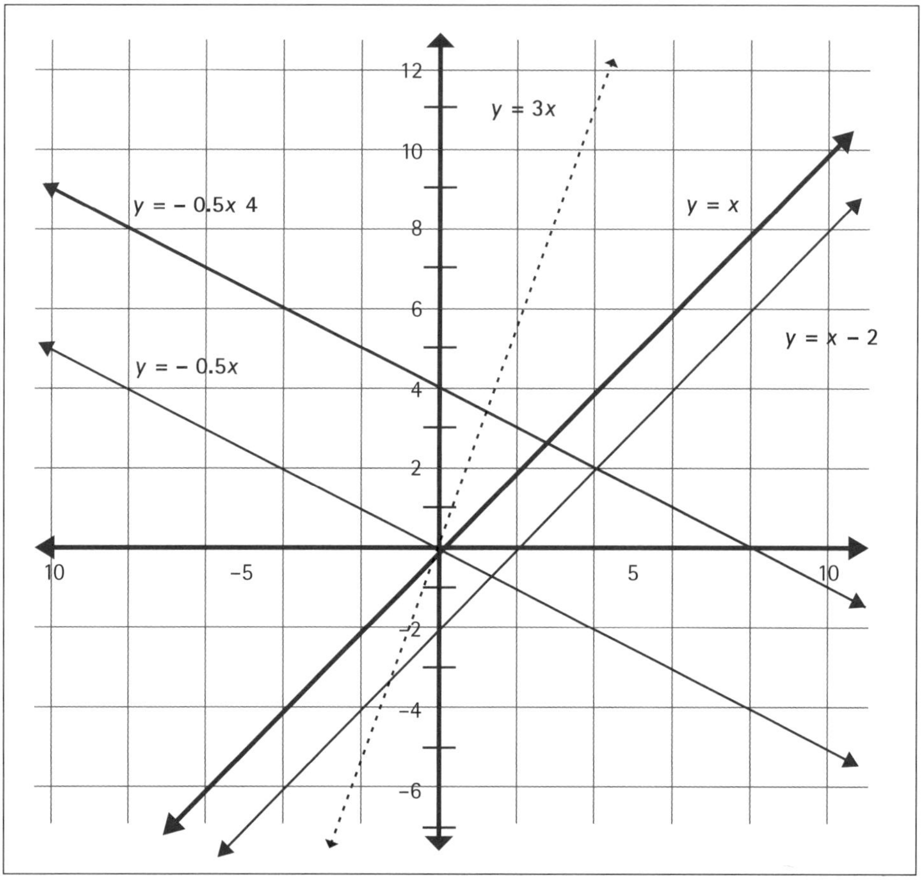

Fig. 1.32. Graphs for linear equations

Functions with changing rates of change

We have explored linear functions and identified linear patterns of change in tables, graphs, and symbolic rules. We now consider other kinds of functions, whose rates of change are not constant. Although these functions do not have constant rates of change as linear functions do, they have rates of change that are predictable, and they can be used to model real-world phenomena and mathematical relationships.

To begin thinking about nonlinear functions, consider Reflect 1.27, which invites you to explore several different relationships and think about their rates of change. Making multiple representations of the relationships helps to develop an overall sense of the underlying patterns of change (Essential Understanding 4*b*).

← ← ←

As shown in the table in figure 1.33, the Painted Cube problem involves several different patterns of change. Suppose that we use the variable n to represent the edge length of a large cube. Consider the functions whose outputs are the numbers of cubes painted on 3,

Essential Understanding 4*b*
Functions can be represented in multiple ways—in algebraic symbols, situations, graphs, verbal descriptions, tables, and so on—and these representations, and the links among them, are useful in analyzing patterns of change.

stop reflect

See Reflect 1.27 on p. 58.

Reflect 1.27

Painted Cube Problem

Investigate what happens when different-sized cubes are constructed from unit cubes, the surface areas of the resulting larger cubes are painted, and then each of the larger cubes is disassembled into its original unit cubes. In each case, how many of the 1 × 1 × 1 cubes are painted on three faces? Two faces? One face? No face? Use tables, graphs, and symbolic rules to explore the relationships involved in this situation. (This problem is adapted from NCTM [1989, p. 99–100]. A similar problem is investigated in Lappan, Fey, Fitzgerald, Friel, and Phillips [2004a, pp. 71–84].)

Dimensions	Number of unit cubes	Number of unit cubes with paint on 3 faces	Number of unit cubes with paint on 2 faces	Number of unit cubes with paint on 1 face	Number of unit cubes with paint on 0 faces
2 × 2 × 2	8	8	0	0	0
3 × 3 × 3	27	8	12	6	1
4 × 4 × 4	64	8	24	24	8
5 × 5 × 5	125	8	36	54	27
6 × 6 × 6	216	8	48	96	64

Fig. 1.33. Number of painted sides in the Painted Cube problem

2, 1, or 0 faces. The table in figure 1.33 shows inputs (n) and outputs for these functions. Notice that, to make sense in this situation, the domain of each of these functions has to be restricted to integers greater than or equal to 2. Thus, the graphs of these functions are actually subsets of the continuous graphs shown in figure 1.34.

Drawing on information from the columns of the table (and the shapes of graphs), we can begin to recognize that f_3 is constant, f_2 is linear, f_1 is quadratic, and f_0 is cubic. Problems such as this one offer opportunities for teachers and students to appreciate that a situation can involve more than one kind of pattern or relationship, to compare and contrast different kinds of rate of change, and to recognize that not all functions are linear. We will now focus our discussion on one of these types of functions—quadratic functions.

Quadratic functions

Essential Understanding 4f. *Quadratic functions are characterized by rates of change that change at a constant rate.*

Situations modeled by quadratic functions are often students' first explicit experience with non-constant rates of change. Unlike linear

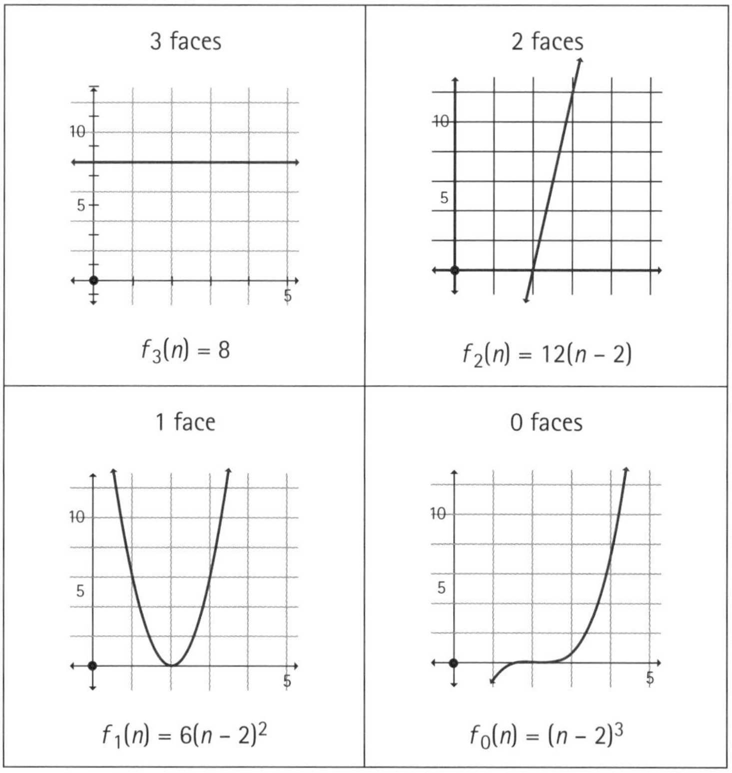

Fig. 1.34. Graphs of functions representing the number of cubes with paint on different number of faces

functions, which have constant rates of change, quadratic functions are characterized by rates of change that are themselves changing at a constant rate. In other words, in a quadratic relationship, the rate of change of the rate of change is constant. This idea is most easily observed in a table of values.

Let's return once more to our service club for an example. Suppose that in the fall, after the service club decides to host a 5K run as a fundraiser, one of the club members proposes using the 5K race as an opportunity to emphasize sportsmanship. This student suggests that the club ask each runner to shake hands with every other runner before the start of the race. Some members of the club like this idea, but others think that so many handshakes could be time-consuming and create a chaotic atmosphere at the starting line. To decide the issue, a club member proposes that the club try to estimate how many handshakes would occur, supposing that 50 runners enter the race. The total number of handshakes depends on, or is a function of, the number of runners in the race. Figure 1.35 presents a table that displays the number of handshakes for 2–7 runners. Reflect 1.28 encourages you to analyze this function.

Number of runners	2	3	4	5	6	7
Number of handshakes	1	3	6	10	15	21

Fig. 1.35. The relationship between the number of runners and the number of handshakes

Reflect 1.28

Consider the table in figure 1.35. If there are only 2 runners, just 1 handshake will occur. If there are 3 runners, 3 handshakes will occur. If there are 4 runners, how many handshakes will occur? If there are 50 runners (the club's estimate), how many handshakes will occur? (This problem is a variation of the widely known Handshake Problem.)

We can understand the pattern of change in this function by looking at the first differences and second differences in the data displayed in the table in figure 1.35. As the number of runners increases from 2 to 3, the number of handshakes increases by 2. As the number of runners increases from 3 to 4, the number of handshakes increases by 3. These increases, or *first differences*, are displayed in figure 1.36.

Number of runners	2	3	4	5	6	7
Number of handshakes	1	3	6	10	15	21
	+2 →	+3 →	+4 →	+5 →	+6 →	

Fig. 1.36. First differences in the relationship between runners and handshakes

In contrast to the first differences in the examples of linear functions that we discussed earlier (for instance, see the example in fig. 1.26), the first differences in this function are not constant. What pattern of change is exhibited in the first differences? As shown in figure 1.37, the *second differences* (in other words, the differences that show the change in the change) are constant. A nonzero constant second difference is characteristic of quadratic functions.

Number of runners	2	3	4	5	6	7
Number of handshakes	1	3	6	10	15	21
	+2 →	+3 →	+4 →	+5 →	+6 →	
		+1 →	+1→	+1→	+1 →	

Fig. 1.37. Constant second differences in the relationship between runners and handshakes

The students in the service club are hoping to determine the number of handshakes that will occur if 50 runners enter the 5K race. After developing a table of values like the one in figure 1.35, the service club members could develop an expression for the number of handshakes completed by n runners in different ways. Suppose that they develop the following expressions

$$\frac{n(n-1)}{2} \quad \text{and} \quad \frac{1}{2}\left(n^2 - n\right).$$

Reflect 1.29 probes the reasoning that the students might have used in generating each of these expressions for the number of handshakes to be exchanged by the runners before the 5K race.

Reflect 1.29

What might have been the service club members' reasoning in developing the expressions

$$\frac{n(n-1)}{2} \quad \text{and} \quad \frac{1}{2}\left(n^2 - n\right)$$

for the number of handshakes to be exchanged before the 5K race? Are the expressions equivalent?

To develop the expression $n(n - 1)/2$, a student might have thought about each of the n runners shaking hands with each of the $n - 1$ other runners (since each runner does not shake his or her own hand), for a total of $n(n - 1)$ handshakes. This method counts each handshake twice (for example, it redundantly counts runner A shaking hands with runner B and runner B shaking hands with runner A as two separate handshakes), so the student needs to divide the expression by 2.

To develop the expression $^1/_2(n^2 - n)$, a student might figure out that n runners will complete n^2 handshakes. She might then decide that since the runners don't shake their own hands, however, there will be n fewer than n^2 handshakes: $n^2 - n$. She then might see that this method counts each handshake twice, so she needs to multiply the expression by $^1/_2$.

When $n = 50$ is substituted into either of the expressions above, we find that the number of handshakes that occur among a group of 50 runners is 1225. That is a lot of handshakes! As discussed previously (in our discussion of Big Idea 1), just because the two expressions produce the same result for $n = 50$ does not mean that they are equivalent. However, when we apply the distributive property to the first expression, $n(n - 1)/2$ yields $(n^2 - n)/2$, an expression that is equivalent to the second expression, $^1/_2(n^2 - n)$. Both of these expressions are equivalent to $^1/_2(n^2) - {}^1/_2 n$. These ideas are based on transformations covered in Essential Understanding 1c.

Big Idea 1

Expressions are foundational for algebra; they serve as building blocks for work with equations and functions.

Essential Understanding 1c
A relatively small number of symbolic transformations can be applied to expressions to yield equivalent expressions.

This handshake situation can be represented by the graph in figure 1.38a. In the particular context that we have been considering, only values of n (number of runners) that are integers greater than or equal to 2 make sense. However, the graph of the handshake relationship is part of the graph corresponding to $h = {}^1/_2(n^2) - {}^1/_2 n$, shown in figure 1.38b. The second graph is a symmetric, almost U-shaped curve.

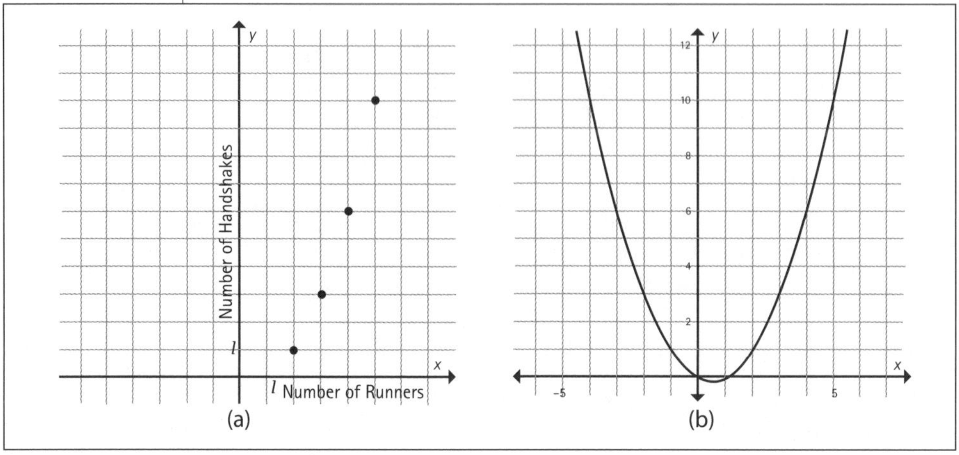

Fig. 1.38. Discrete points (a) and the parabolic graph (b) corresponding to $h = 1/2(n^2) - 1/2n$, the number of handshakes as a function of the number of runners

The graph of any function with a rule of the type $f(x) = ax^2 + bx + c$, for nonzero a, has the general shape of the graph in figure 1.38b and is called a *parabola*. Parabolas are useful for modeling many real-world situations, including those that involve the height of a projectile over time. Reflect 2.3 explores a situation of this type later.

Exponential functions

Essential Understanding 4g. *In exponential growth, the rate of change increases over the domain, but in exponential decay, the rate of change decreases over the domain.*

Exponential functions model various real-world situations in which amounts increase or decrease at a rate proportional to the amount present. Population growth over time and depreciation in value over time are both examples of exponential functions. Like quadratic functions, exponential functions have a rate of change that is not constant (as in linear functions) but changes. In exponential growth, the rate of change increases over time, but in exponential decay, the rate of change decreases over time.

Let's move to a situation outside the fundraising context and consider a problem situation that is common in middle school curriculum program, namely, the growth of different plants. (See, for example, the unit "Growth" in *Mathematics in Context* [Roodhardt et al. 1998].) Suppose that the height of plant A in millimeters can be described by $h(t) = 10 + 12t$, where t is time in weeks, and the height of plant B can be described by $g(t) = 10 \cdot (2)^t$. The plants' heights over several weeks appear in the tables in figure 1.39.

Plant A	
t	$h(t)$
0	10
1	22
2	34
3	46
4	58
5	70

Plant B	
t	$g(t)$
0	10
1	20
2	40
3	80
4	160
5	320

Fig. 1.39. Tables representing plant heights (approximate) over time

We have already explored the first type of function, a linear function, in which the rate of change is constant. As each week passes, the height of plant A increases by 12 millimeters. We can express this change by describing one value of the function in terms of the preceding value. If we move from the first term (10) to the second term (22), we can express the relationship as $10 + 12 = 22$. Similarly, we can move from the second to the third term with $22 + 12 = 34$. This type of relationship is called *recursion* because we rely on knowing one value to find the next value. We can write the following to express the growth of plant A recursively: $h(t + 1) = h(t) + 12$. Expressing the plant's growth in this way helps to draw attention to the constant rate of change in the function, which is also displayed in the graph in figure 1.40. Reflect 1.30 focuses on the nature of the growth of plant B.

Reflect 1.30

What pattern of change is involved with the growth of plant B? Try to develop a recursive way to express the growth of plant B.

The function describing plant B's growth over time is nonlinear and has a unique pattern of change. As each week passes, the height of the plant doubles. This nonlinear function is called *exponential* because the variable t appears only in the exponent of the rule for the height. In exponential functions involving time, the value of the output variable at time $t + 1$ can be calculated by multiplying the value at time t by a constant factor. For example, in the case of plant B, we can find $g(5)$ by multiplying $g(4)$ by the constant factor 2:

$$g(5) = 2 \cdot g(4)$$

$$g(5) = 2 \cdot 160$$

$$g(5) = 320$$

In general, $g(t + 1) = 2 \cdot g(t)$. As shown in the table in figure 1.39, the height of plant B doubles each week. Whereas the first differences in plant A's heights in the table are constant (+12), the first differences in plant B's heights (+10, +20, +40, ...) are constantly increasing (by a factor of 2). Plant B's rate of growth becomes faster as time passes.

The graphs in figure 1.40 illustrate the contrast in appearance between a graph of a linear function and a graph of an exponential function. The graph corresponding to the exponential function $g(t) = 10 \cdot (2)^t$ is a smooth curve that lies completely above the horizontal axis. Because the rate of change increases over time, the graph is not a line but an increasing curve. To explore the pattern of change in exponential functions further, consider Reflect 1.31.

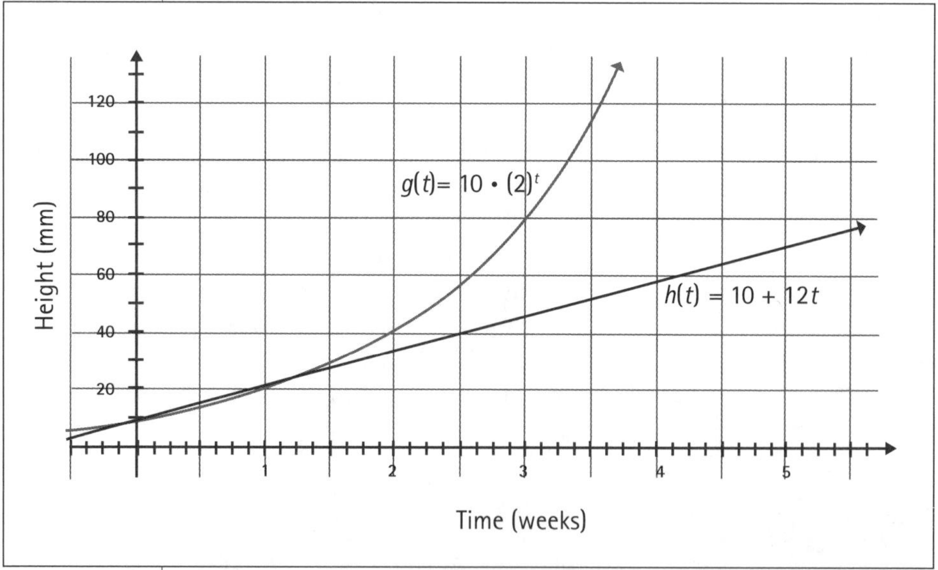

Fig. 1.40. Graphs representing plant heights over time

Reflect 1.31

Suppose that 32 teams enter an elimination soccer tournament. Consider the exponential function, $k(t) = 32 \cdot (^1/_2)^t$ describing the number of teams that remain in the tournament after t rounds. What is the pattern of change in this function?

Like the function g, which we used to describe the height of plant B at the end of t weeks, the function k, which describes the number of teams remaining in the tournament after t rounds, is exponential. At the beginning of the tournament, 32 teams are participating. After teams compete in the first round of the tournament, only half of the teams remain. In other words, the initial number of teams is multiplied by 1/2, leaving 16 teams to compete in the second round of the tournament. In general, we can say $k(t + 1) = {}^1/_2 \cdot k(t)$. After four rounds, two teams will compete to determine the winning team in round 5. This pattern of exponential decay appears in the table in figure 1.41.

t	$k(t)$
0	32
1	16
2	8
3	4
4	2
5	1

Fig. 1.41. The pattern of exponential decay in the soccer tournament situation

The exponential decay in the tournament situation is illustrated in the graph in figure 1.42. Whereas the plant function $g(t) = 10 \cdot (2)^t$ models a rate of growth that becomes faster as time passes, the tournament function $k(t) = 32 \cdot ({}^1/_2)^t$ models a rate of decay that becomes slower over time. Notice that, in the soccer tournament situation, it does not make sense to analyze the function beyond $t = 5$, because at the end of the fifth round, there is a winning team. If we consider the function $k(t) = 32 \cdot ({}^1/_2)^t$ more generally, as a function over the real numbers, we can see that as t increases, the function decreases, and its graph is closer and closer to the horizontal axis as we look at it from left to right, but it never touches the axis. In other words, like all exponential functions of the form $f(x) = ab^x$ where a and b are real numbers and $b > 0$, the graph of the function $k(t) = 32 \cdot ({}^1/_2)^t$ has an *asymptote* (a line that the graph approaches but never intersects) at the horizontal axis. This makes sense because there is no value for t that would make the function expression $32 \cdot ({}^1/_2)^t$ equal to zero.

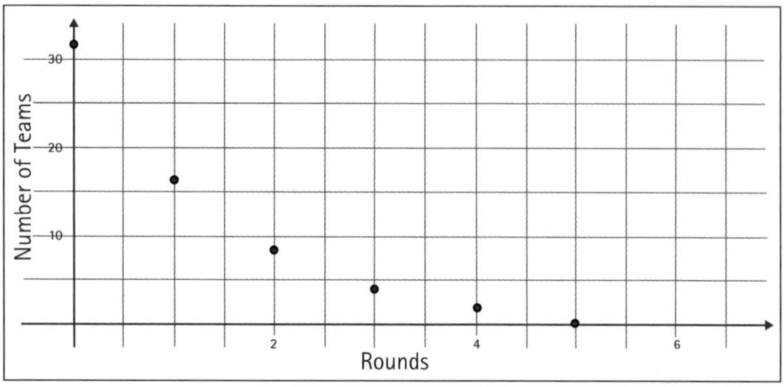

Fig. 1.42. A graph showing exponential decay in the soccer tournament situation

Solving Equations: Big Idea 5

Big Idea 5. *General algorithms exist for solving many kinds of equations; these algorithms are broadly applicable for solving a wide range of similar equations. However, for some problems or situations, alternatives to these general algorithms may be more elegant, efficient, or informative.*

In our discussion of Big Idea 4, we explored symbolic, graphical, and tabular representations of functions in a variety of situations. In some of these situations, we were interested in determining the output value for a function for a given input value (or the input value for a given output). Similarly, in our earlier discussion in Big Idea 3, our investigation of a hypothetical situation led us to an equation to solve. We supposed that students in a school service club were considering joining one of two national service clubs, Kids Help and United Service, and we discovered that the students could solve the equation $10x + 20 = 5x + 50$ to determine when membership in each service club might be a better deal. Solving algebraic equations is very useful in these kinds of situations. In examining Big Idea 3, we established that the process of solving an equation involves applying symbolic transformations that preserve the equivalence of the two expressions in the equation. In examining Big Idea 5, we return to symbolic methods of equation solving and consider the different ways that both linear and quadratic equations can be solved.

Note that in our presentation of Big Idea 5, we have deliberately chosen to focus on methods for symbolic manipulation that are not explicitly linked to a familiar context. Big Idea 5 is fundamentally about the symbolic methods that we use in solving equations. In discussing Big Idea 5, we invite you to make meaning of the strategies that we can use to solve equations symbolically—to consider whether general algorithms exist and whether alternative symbolic methods exist and under what circumstances these alternative methods might be useful or appropriate. With these goals in mind, begin by considering Reflect 1.32, which investigates whether you believe that there is a standard way to solve all linear equations.

Big Idea 4

Functions provide a means for describing and understanding relationships between variables. They can have multiple representations—in algebraic symbols, situations, graphs, verbal descriptions, tables, and so on—and they can be classified into different families with similar patterns of change.

Big Idea 3

The equals sign indicates that two expressions are equivalent. It can also be used in defining or naming a single expression or function rule.

Reflect 1.32

Is there a standard method or algorithm that you use to teach students to solve all linear equations? Do you teach students alternatives to this algorithm? Why or why not?

A general algorithm for solving linear equations

Essential Understanding 5a. *A general algorithm exists for solving linear equations. This algorithm is broadly applicable and reasonably efficient.*

A general and quite useful algorithm exists for solving linear equations. Stated in its most general form, the algorithm consists of the steps shown in figure 1.43, although it may not be necessary to use all steps for all linear equations. This algorithm is widely taught in the United States.

Equation to solve:	$3(x + 2) + 4x + 7 = 5(2x - 1) + 4 - x$
1. Apply distributive property to one or both expressions to clear parentheses:	$3x + 6 + 4x + 7 = 10x - 5 + 4 - x$
2. Collect like variable terms and constants in each expression:	$7x + 13 = 9x - 1$
3. Isolate variable terms on one side of the equation and constant terms on the other side:	$-2x = -14$
4. Divide both sides by the coefficient of the variable term to arrive at the equation's solution:	$x = 7$

Fig. 1.43. Steps in the general algorithm for solving linear equations

First, we apply the distributive property to either or both expressions. Informally, this application of the distributive property has the effect of *clearing*, or eliminating, the parentheses. More substantively, distributing first makes it easier to identify like variable and constant terms, in anticipation of the second step of the algorithm.

Second, we collect like variables and constants in each expression. Mathematically, collecting like terms involves combining like variable and constant terms in each expression by using the distributive property and perhaps the associative and commutative properties. In the example in figure 1.43, $3x$ and $4x$ are like terms in the expression on the left side of the equation and can be combined by applying the distributive property: $3x + 4x$ is $(3 + 4)x$, or $7x$.

Third, using the properties of equality, we isolate variable terms on one side of the equation and constant terms on the other side. As a result of collecting like terms (step 2), we transform each expression in figure 1.43 so that it has, at most, a single variable term and a single constant term; it is of the form $ax + b = cx + d$, where a, b, c, and d are real numbers and ac is not 0. Isolating the variable and constant terms (step 3) involves adding either $-cx - b$ or $-ax - d$ to both expressions.

Finally, we divide both sides of the equation by the coefficient of the variable term, if it is not 0. Our work in step 3 transformed the equation to the form $rx = s$, so we can solve for x (step 4) by dividing both expressions in the equation by r (or multiplying by the reciprocal of r).

Note that not all equations require the use of all steps in the algorithm. For example, to solve the equation $3x + 2x + 7 = 13x + 3$, we can start the algorithm at the second step. Similarly, to solve the equation $5x + 1 = 2x + 7$, we can start the algorithm at the third step.

Introductory algebra texts around the world generally teach an algorithm for solving linear equations. It is important to recognize that nothing about the particular algorithm described above is mathematically sacred. There is considerable variation in the algorithms taught for solving linear equations. Some texts modify the algorithm in figure 1.43 slightly by inserting an initial step that calls for multiplying both expressions by a constant to clear any fractional coefficients that may be present. Figure 1.44 shows another variant that is seen in several countries; this alternative algorithm is equally efficient but subtly different from the one typically taught in the United States.

Equation to solve:	$3(x + 2) + 4x + 7 = 5(2x - 1) + 4 - x$
1. Apply distributive property to one or both expressions to clear parentheses:	$3x + 6 + 4x + 7 = 10x - 5 + 4 - x$
2. To both expressions: Act as though to add the additive inverse of all variable terms in one expression and the additive inverse of all constant terms in the other expression:	$3x + 4x - 10x + x = -5 + 4 - 6 - 7$
3. Collect like variable terms and constants in each expression:	$-2x = -14$
4. Divide both sides by the coefficient of the variable term to arrive at the equation's solution:	$x = 7$

Fig. 1.44. Steps in an alternate algorithm for solving linear equations

Symbolic, graphical, and numerical solution methods

Essential Understanding 5b. *Linear equations can be solved by symbolic, graphical, and numerical methods. On some occasions and in some contexts, one solution method may be more elegant, efficient, or informative than another.*

As the existence of multiple algorithms for solving linear equations suggests, there are many ways to solve linear equations, including several efficient and broadly applicable algorithms. So, although the axioms of equality provide guidance about the operations that can be applied to equations to preserve equivalence, these axioms do not provide strategic guidance as to which operations might be helpful (and in what order) in solving a given equation in a particular set of circumstances. Reflect 1.33 invites you to consider several different solutions to a linear equation and to think about the efficiency of each one.

Reflect 1.33

Consider the equation $3x - 8 = 8x + 12$ and the three solutions below. Compare and contrast the solution methods and evaluate the efficiency of each method.

Method A	Method B	Method C
$3x - 8 = 8x + 12$	$3x - 8 = 8x + 12$	$3x - 8 = 8x + 12$
$3x = 8x + 20$	$-5x - 8 = 12$	$3x - 8 - 8x - 12 = 0$
$-5x = 20$	$-5x = 20$	$3x - 8 - 8x = 12$
$x = -4$	$x = -4$	$3x - 8x = 20$
		$-5x = 20$
		$x = -4$

Some ways of solving equations may appear to be different from the efficient algorithm only in trivial ways, whereas other ways may be significantly more (or less) efficient or useful. The difference between methods A and B in Reflect 1.33 might seem somewhat insignificant. In method A, 8 and then $-8x$ are added to both expressions; in method B, this order is reversed ($-8x$ and then 8 are added to both expressions). Despite this difference, one could argue that methods A and B are equally efficient (for example, they take the same number of steps). Method C, although a mathematically correct and legitimate way to solve this equation, is arguably less efficient than either of the other methods.

Of all possible strategies for solving a given equation, the strategy that is most appropriate will depend on a number of factors, possibly including the structure of the equation (including the value of its constants and coefficients, or the position of terms within the equation), and the problem solver's goals (whether efficiency is a top priority or whether it is more important to avoid making any mistakes, for example). Some people use the term *elegant* to describe those strategies that are especially appropriate, useful, efficient, or informative in solving a given equation. (This same point applies to equations that are not linear, but we focus only on linear equations here.) Consider in Reflect 1.34 what it might mean for a strategy to be most appropriate for solving a given equation.

Reflect 1.34

Consider the equation $3(x + 1) = 15$. How would you solve this equation? Think about the steps that you would take, and why you would take them. Then compare and contrast the two strategies presented below. Which strategy is more efficient, and why?

Standard Algorithm	Alternative Strategy
$3(x + 1) = 15$	$3(x + 1) = 15$
$3x + 3 = 15$	$x + 1 = 5$
$3x = 12$	$x = 4$
$x = 4$	

In solving the equation $3(x + 1) = 15$, it may be advantageous to divide both expressions by 3 as a first step rather than distributing, as step 1 in the algorithm commonly taught in the United States would suggest. Arguably, this alternative solution strategy is more efficient than the U.S. standard algorithm. Similarly, the alternative solutions shown for two equations in Reflect 1.35 may be more efficient than the U.S. standard algorithm. Take a moment to consider why.

← ← ←

stop reflect

See Reflect 1.35 on p. 72.

It is advantageous for students to develop fluency in the use of multiple strategies for solving equations and to develop the ability to select the most appropriate strategy for a given problem. Understanding the process of equation solving includes being flexible in the use of multiple equation-solving strategies.

Solving quadratic equations

Essential Understanding 5c. *Quadratic equations can be solved by using graphs and tables and by applying an algorithm that involves* completing the square. *This algorithm, when expressed in a more compact form, is also known as the* quadratic formula.

As we discussed for solving linear equations, there is a standard algorithm for solving quadratic equations, but there are also

Reflect 1.35

What makes the alternative strategies shown below more efficient for solving these equations?

Standard Algorithm	Alternative Strategy
$2(x + 1) + 5(x + 1) = 14$	$2(x + 1) + 5(x + 1) = 14$
$2x + 2 + 5x + 5 = 14$	$7(x + 1) = 14$
$7x + 7 = 14$	$x + 1 = 2$
$7x = 7$	$x = 1$
$x = 1$	
$\frac{1}{3}(x + 3) + \frac{2}{3}(x + 3) = 8$	$\frac{1}{3}(x + 3) + \frac{2}{3}(x + 3) = 8$
$\frac{1}{3}x + 1 + \frac{2}{3}x + 2 = 8$	$x + 3 = 8$
$x + 3 = 8$	$x = 5$
$x = 5$	

several other methods for doing so, as Essential Understanding 5c asserts. In this section, we will explore this algorithm, which involves the process known as *completing the square*, and its more compact form, known as the *quadratic formula*. We will also explore alternative solution methods using graphs. First, take the opportunity offered by Reflect 1.36 to think about the methods that you use in teaching students how to work with quadratic equations.

Reflect 1.36

How do you teach students to solve quadratic equations? Do you help them learn multiple methods for solving quadratics? Are some methods more useful than others?

As was true in the case of linear equations, when we solve a quadratic equation, we are interested in finding the value(s) of the variable for which the expressions in the equation have the same value. Recall a problem context that we found useful in exploring Big Idea 4—the number of handshakes among runners in a 5K race. In Reflect 1.28 and 1.29, we determined that symbolically the quadratic relationship between the number of runners (n) and the number of handshakes (h) could be written as $h = {}^1/_2\, n^2 - {}^1/_2\, n$. If we were interested in learning how many runners were in the race when the total number of handshakes was 300, we could write the quadratic equation ${}^1/_2\, n^2 - {}^1/_2\, n = 300$.

Solving this equation means finding the value(s) of n so that $1/2\ n^2 - 1/2\ n$ is equal to 300. As we discussed in connection with Big Idea 3, we can try to find these values by using tables or graphs, by reasoning through the context, or by working symbolically. As equations become increasingly complex, however, we tend to rely more on graphical and symbolic methods for solving them.

The graphs in figure 1.45 show us two points at which the line $h = 300$ intersects the curve $h = 1/2\ n^2 - 1/2\ n$. However, only one of these points, (25, 300), makes sense as a solution in the handshake context. (We cannot have a negative number of runners, but it can be easier to graph the continuous function than the function for the handshake situation. The domain of this function is the nonnegative integers, so the point (–24, 300) does not make sense.) Looking at the graph in figure 1.45, we can see that for an exchange of 300 handshakes, there must be 25 runners.

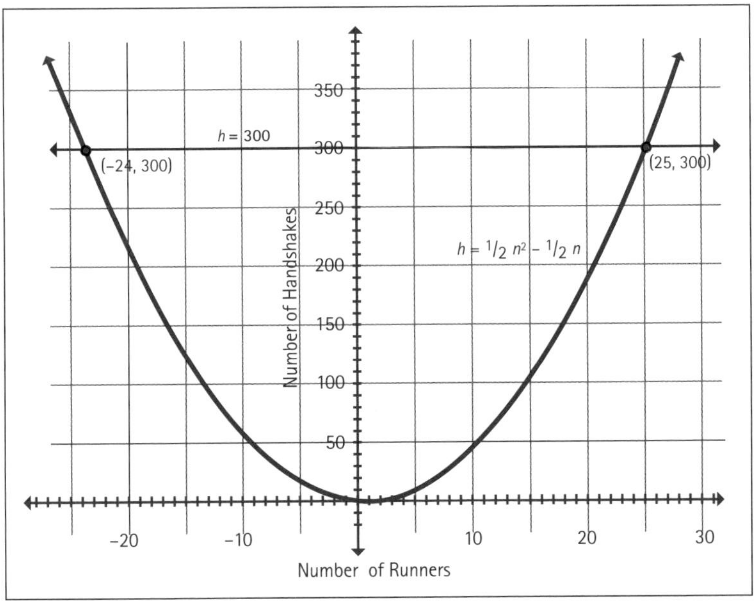

Fig. 1.45. Graphs of $h = 1/2\ n^2 - 1/2\ n$ (the number of handshakes as a function of the number of runners) and $h = 300$ (300 handshakes)

A well-known way to solve a quadratic equation such as $1/2\ n^2 - 1/2\ n = 300$ symbolically is by using what is typically referred to as the *quadratic formula*. The quadratic formula states that the solution(s) x_1 and x_2 to a quadratic equation of the form $ax^2 + bx + c = 0$, where a is not equal to 0, are the following:

$$x_1 = \frac{-b + \sqrt{b^2 - 4ac}}{2a}$$

$$x_2 = \frac{-b - \sqrt{b^2 - 4ac}}{2a}$$

Big Idea 4

Functions provide a means for describing and understanding relationships between variables. They can have multiple representations—in algebraic symbols, situations, graphs, verbal descriptions, tables, and so on—and they can be classified into different families *with similar patterns of change.*

Big Idea 3

The equals sign indicates that two expressions are equivalent. It can also be used in defining or naming a single expression or function rule.

We can use the quadratic formula to solve $1/2\, n^2 - 1/2\, n = 300$ as follows:

$$\frac{1}{2}n^2 - \frac{1}{2}n - 300 = 0$$

$$n = \frac{1}{2} \pm \sqrt{\frac{1}{4} + 600}$$

$$n = \frac{1}{2} \pm \frac{1}{2}\sqrt{2401}$$

$$n = \frac{1}{2} \pm \frac{1}{2} \cdot 49$$

$$n_1 = 25 \text{ and } n_2 = -24$$

Notice that these solutions correspond to the horizontal coordinates of the two points of intersection of the graphs of figure 1.45.

The quadratic formula is rather cumbersome to remember but is applicable to all quadratic equations. The expression under the radical sign, $b^2 - 4ac$, is known as the *discriminant.* It provides information that enables us to discern, or discriminate, the nature of the solutions. If the value of the discriminant is 0, the quadratic equation has only one solution, and this solution is a real number. If the discriminant is less than 0, the quadratic equation has no real solutions. If the discriminant is positive, the quadratic equation has two real solutions. Why does the discriminant indicate the nature of the solutions of a quadratic function? We will return to this question later, when we have filled in some important details. Meanwhile, figure 1.46 shows graphs of quadratic functions with (*a*) one zero, (*b*) no real zeros, and (*c*) two real zeros. The *zeros* of a function are the solutions of the equation that states that the output of the function is 0.

Big Idea 3

The equals sign indicates that two expressions are equivalent. The equals sign can also be used in defining or naming a single expression or function rule.

Where does the quadratic formula come from? It is helpful to answer this question by first considering a quadratic equation of the form $x^2 = 4$. Recall from our discussion of Big Idea 3 that we solve equations symbolically by applying symbolic transformations that preserve the equivalence of the two expressions in the equation. We discussed some of these symbolic transformations, including the addition property of equality (which holds that we can add a constant to both expressions) and the multiplication property of equality (which holds that we can multiply both expressions by a constant). When we work with quadratic equations, we can use another symbolic transformation that ensures the equivalence of the two new expressions—taking the principal square root of each expression.

In our earlier discussion of transformations that preserve the equivalence of two expressions, we focused on properties of operations such as the distributive and the commutative properties. Square roots provide us with another powerful kind of symbolic transformation, in which we apply to each expression a relation

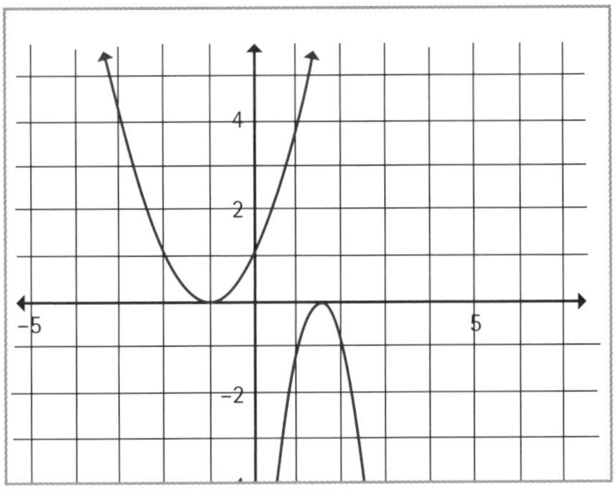

a. One real zero (discriminant is 0)

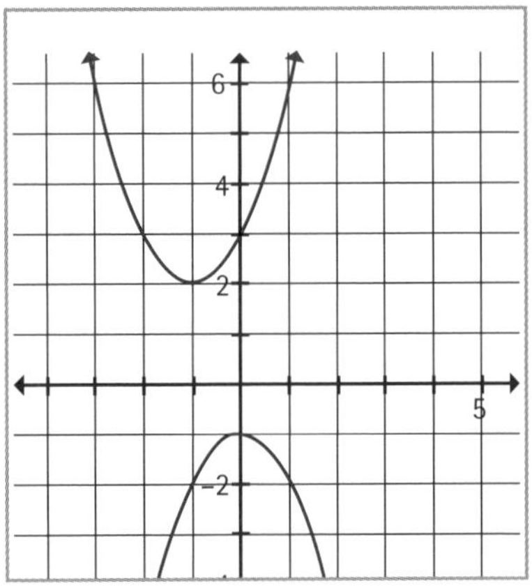

b. No real zeros (discriminant is negative)

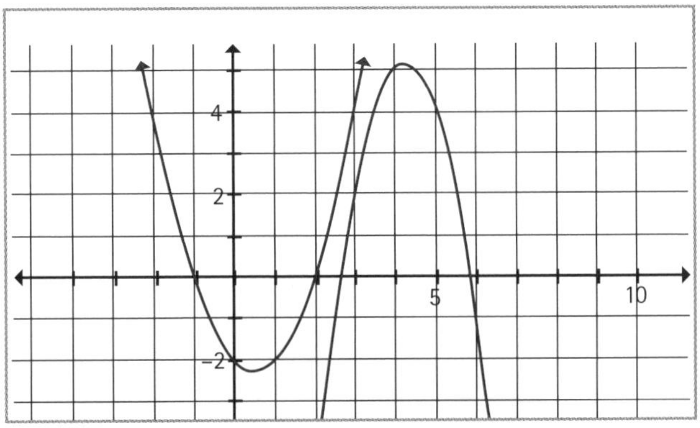

c. Two real zeros (discriminant is positive)

Fig. 1.46. Graphs of quadratic functions with (*a*) one zero, (*b*) no real zeros, and (*c*) two real zeros

that is not a function. It is important to be aware of possible unexpected consequences when we apply a relation that is not a function to equivalent expressions.

The square root of a number x is defined as any number r such that $r^2 = x$. All positive real numbers have two square roots; for example, the square roots of 4 are 2 and −2. Generally, when we write $\sqrt{4}$ we are referring to the principal square root of 4, which is the nonnegative square root; the principal square root of 4 is 2. But when we apply the symbolic transformation of taking the square root of each expression in an equation, we are working with square roots more broadly and not merely with the principal square root. When we take the square root of both expressions in the case of our quadratic equation $x^2 = 4$, because $\sqrt{x^2}$ is $|x|$, we obtain

Chapter 2 discusses taking the logarithm of both expressions in an equation. This transformation involves applying a function on both sides of the equals sign but introduces other challenges.

$$\sqrt{x^2} = \sqrt{4}$$
$$|x| = 2$$
$$x = \pm 2.$$

Taking the square root of both expressions in a quadratic equation is a very useful transformation. If we can use other symbolic transformations to rewrite a quadratic equation in the form $x^2 = c$, then we can easily arrive at the solution by taking the square root of each expression. For example, given the quadratic equation $(x + 4)^2 = 25$, we can take the square root of both expressions:

$$(x + 4)^2 = 25$$
$$\sqrt{(x+4)^2} = \sqrt{25}$$
$$|\, x + 4 \,| = 5$$
$$x + 4 = 5, \text{ so } x = 1$$
$$x + 4 = -5, \text{ so } x = -9$$

Consider the quadratic equation $x^2 + 2x = 8$. The expression $x^2 + 2x$ is very similar to the expression $x^2 + 2x + 1$, which we can rewrite as $(x + 1)^2$. To transform $x^2 + 2x$ into $x^2 + 2x + 1$, we can add 1 to both expressions by the addition property of equality:

$$x^2 + 2x + 1 = 8 + 1$$

We can then rewrite the quadratic equation and solve it as follows:

$$(x + 1)^2 = 9$$
$$\sqrt{(x+1)^2} = \sqrt{9}$$
$$|\, x + 1 \,| = 3$$
$$x + 1 = 3, \text{ so } x = 2$$
$$x + 1 = -3, \text{ so } x = -4$$

This algorithm, in which we apply symbolic transformations to a quadratic equation so that we can rewrite it in the form $x^2 = c$ and then solve by taking the square root of both expressions, involves *completing the square*. Reflect 1.37 invites you to consider a geometric interpretation of completing the square.

stop reflect →

See Reflect 1.37 on p. 77.

→ → →

We can represent the quadratic equation $x^2 + 2x = 8$ geometrically, by starting with a square with a side length of x, as shown in figure 1.47. The area of that square is x^2.

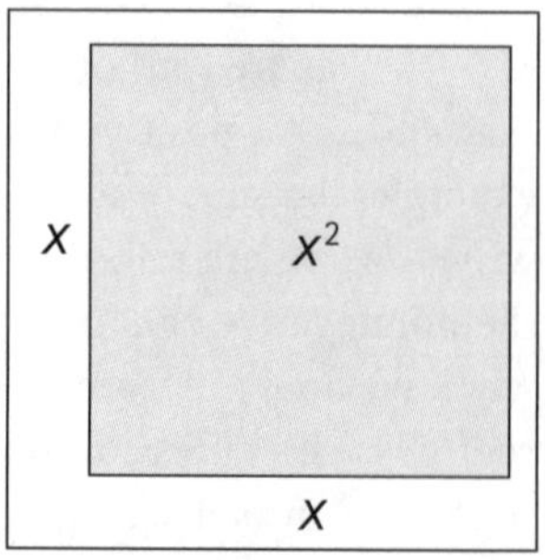

Fig. 1.47. A square with an area of x^2

The next term in the equation, $2x$, is equivalent to $x + x$. We can view this term as the sum of the areas of two rectangular regions such as those shown in figure 1.48. Each

Reflect 1.37

In your instruction, you might use rectangles like those shown below to guide your students through the process of completing the square.

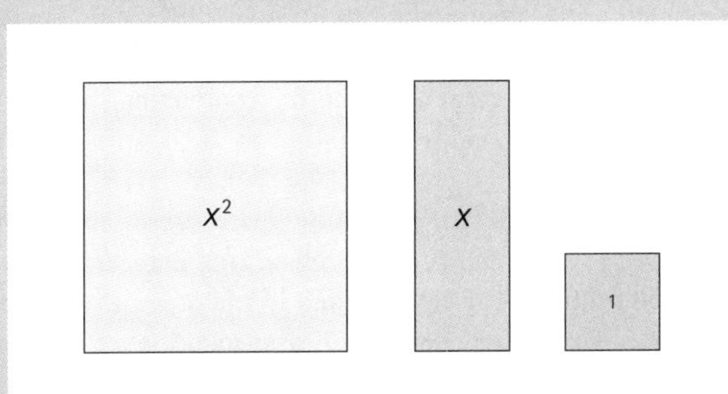

Think about such rectangles and their meaning in the process of completing the square in the case of the quadratic equation just discussed: $x^2 + 2x = 8$.

of these rectangles has dimensions 1 by x and therefore has an area of x square units.

What do we need to add to the figure so that we can complete the square? The missing region from figure 1.48 is a 1-by-1 square with an area of 1. Figure 1.49 shows a square with side lengths of $x + 1$ units, whose area is $x^2 + 2x + 1$.

The additive identity property ensures that $x^2 + 2x$ is equivalent to $x^2 + 2x + 1 + (-1)$ or $x^2 + 2x + 1 - 1$. We can now think of $x^2 + 2x$ as $(x+1)^2 - 1$. To solve $x^2 + 2x = 8$, we can proceed as follows:

$$x^2 + 2x = 8$$
$$(x+1)^2 - 1 = 8$$
$$(x+1)^2 = 9$$

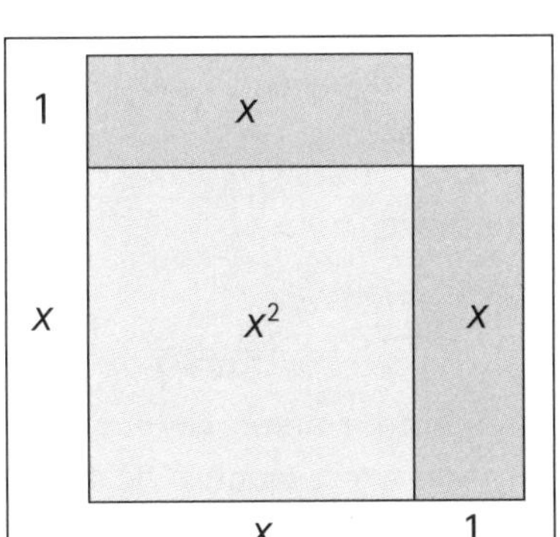

Fig. 1.48. The addition of two rectangular regions representing $2x$

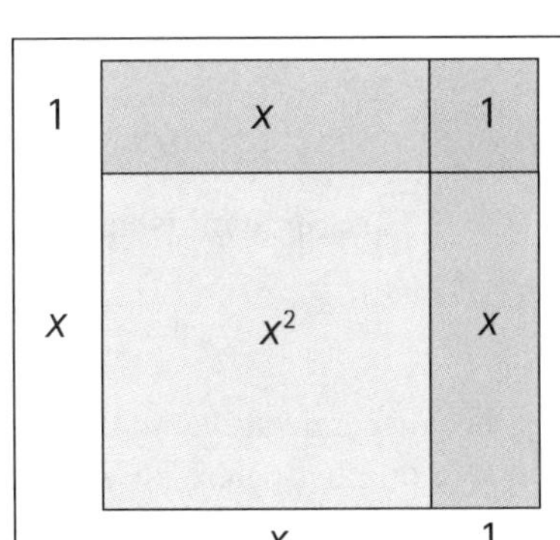

Fig. 1.49. A square with an area of $x^2 + 2x + 1$

Phelps and Edwards (2010) extend the idea of completing the square in intriguing ways.

As shown above, we can take the square root of each expression to obtain $|x + 1| = 3$, so $x = -4$ and $x = 2$.

Completing the square is a broadly applicable algorithm that yields the solution for all quadratic equations. Figure 1.50 shows the completing the square algorithm for solving the quadratic equation $3x^2 + 6x - 4 = 0$ and for the more general quadratic equation $ax^2 + bx + c = 0$. Note that applying the completing the square algorithm to the general quadratic equation $ax^2 + bx + c = 0$ yields the quadratic formula.

We can now answer the question posed earlier about *why* the value of the discriminant $b^2 - 4ac$ tells us the nature of the zeros of a quadratic function (see figure 1.46). In the process of completing the square to solve the general quadratic equation $ax^2 + bx + c = 0$ (see the right-hand column in figure 1.50), we developed the following equation:

$$\left(x+\frac{b}{2a}\right)^2=\left(\frac{b^2-4ac}{4a^2}\right)$$

Notice that the discriminant is the numerator of the expression on the right side of this equation. Let's look more closely at this step to investigate the role of the discriminant in determining the nature of the solution(s).

The square of any real number is nonnegative. Assuming that a is not equal to 0 (if a were 0, then $ax^2 + bx + c = 0$ would not be a quadratic equation but simply $bx + c = 0$), we know that a^2 and $4a^2$ are positive. So a way to interpret the equation above is

$$\left(x+\frac{b}{2a}\right)^2 = \text{discriminant} \div \text{a positive number.}$$

If the discriminant equals 0, then this equation becomes

$$\left(x+\frac{b}{2a}\right)^2=0,$$

in which case the equation has only one solution,

$$x=-\frac{b}{2a}.$$

If the discriminant is negative, we are left with

$$\left(x+\frac{b}{2a}\right)^2 = \text{a negative number}$$

because a negative number divided by a positive number is a negative number. There are no real numbers that when squared yield a negative number, so there are no real solutions when the discriminant is negative. Finally, when the discriminant is positive,

$$\left(x+\frac{b}{2a}\right)^2 = \text{a positive number,}$$

$3x^2 + 6x - 4 = 0$	$ax^2 + bx + c = 0$
$3x^2 + 6x = 4$	$ax^2 + bx = -c$
$3(x^2 + 2x) = 4$	$a\left(x^2 + \left(\frac{b}{a}\right)x\right) = -c$
$3(x^2 + 2x + 1) = 4 + 3$	$a\left(x^2 + \left(\frac{b}{a}\right)x + \left(\frac{b}{2a}\right)^2\right) = -c + \frac{b^2}{4a}$
	$a\left(x + \frac{b}{2a}\right)^2 = -c + \frac{b^2}{4a}$
$3(x + 1)^2 = 7$	$a\left(x + \frac{b}{2a}\right)^2 = \left(\frac{b^2 - 4ac}{4a}\right)$
$(x+1)^2 = \frac{7}{3}$	$\left(x + \frac{b}{2a}\right)^2 = \left(\frac{b^2 - 4ac}{4a^2}\right)$
$\sqrt{(x+1)^2} = \sqrt{\frac{7}{3}}$	$\sqrt{\left(x + \frac{b}{2a}\right)^2} = \sqrt{\frac{-c}{a} + \frac{b^2}{4a^2}}$
$\lvert x+1 \rvert = \sqrt{\frac{7}{3}}$	$\left\lvert x + \frac{b}{2a} \right\rvert = \sqrt{\frac{-c}{a} + \frac{b^2}{4a^2}}$
$x+1 = \sqrt{\frac{7}{3}}$, so $x = \sqrt{\frac{7}{3}} - 1$	$x = \frac{-b}{2a} \pm \sqrt{\frac{-c}{a} + \frac{b^2}{4a^2}}$
$x+1 = -\sqrt{\frac{7}{3}}$, so $x = -\sqrt{\frac{7}{3}} - 1$	$x = \frac{-b}{2a} \pm \sqrt{\frac{b^2 - 4ac}{2a}}$

Fig. 1.50. Solving quadratic equations by completing the square

meaning that

$$x + \frac{b}{2a}$$

can be the positive or the negative square root of

$$\frac{b^2 - 4ac}{4a^2},$$

or

$$x = \frac{-b}{2a} \pm \sqrt{\frac{b^2 - 4ac}{2a}}.$$

Conclusion

In this chapter, we have developed five big ideas, with associated essential understandings, which are central to teachers' understanding of expressions, equations, and functions. You may find it useful at this point to revisit the list of essential understandings at the beginning of chapter 1 and consider the ways in which your views of algebra have changed. Reflect 1.38 offers you this opportunity.

Reflect 1.38

Read the list of big ideas and essential understandings presented at the beginning of this chapter. Try to identify some specific ways in which your understanding has changed, even if those changes seem subtle. What surprises, if any, have you had about your knowledge of the mathematics that you teach? As you think about changes in your understanding, also consider (and discuss with colleagues, if possible) how your new knowledge will affect your teaching of algebra.

Algebraic ideas are tremendously challenging for both students and teachers. Perhaps for many years you have taught a method for completing the square without being quite sure why the method makes sense or why it is valuable. Or perhaps you have always taught the idea of slope with an emphasis on the formula "change in y over change in x," and now you have a better sense of what this ratio means with respect to the relationship between variables in a linear function. Or maybe you are a beginning teacher and are realizing that the way you learned about solving linear equations as a student is not as meaningful as it could be. These are all examples of changes in understanding that have the potential to contribute to changes in classroom instruction.

The ideas that we have developed in this chapter are intended to improve teachers' ability to support students' learning about algebra in grades 6–8. The particular essential understandings that we have explored provide a basis for classroom instruction that supports the recommendations in *Principles and Standards for School Mathematics* (National Council of Teachers of Mathematics 2000). Figure 1.51 displays the expectations that compose the Algebra Standard for all students in grades 6–8. In chapter 1, we have developed mathematical ideas that support instruction about all of the elements in this list of expectations.

Big Idea 1

Expressions. *Expressions are foundational for algebra; they serve as building blocks for work with equations and functions.*

A grasp of the big ideas and essential understandings in this book will also enhance teachers' abilities to enact state or district curriculum standards. For example, your state may have recently adopted the Common Core State Standards (CCSSI 2010). The Standards for Mathematical Content outlined for grades 6–8

Algebra Standard	Expectations *In grades 6–8 all students should–*
Understand patterns, relations, and functions	• represent, analyze, and generalize a variety of patterns with tables, graphs, words, and, when possible, symbolic rules; • relate and compare different forms of representation for a relationship; • identify functions as linear or nonlinear and contrast their properties from tables, graphs, or equations.
Represent and analyze mathematical situations and structures using algebraic symbols	• develop an initial conceptual understanding of different uses of variables; • explore relationships between symbolic expressions and graphs of lines, paying particular attention to the meaning of intercept and slope; • use symbolic algebra to represent situations and to solve problems, especially those that involve linear relationships; • recognize and generate equivalent forms for simple algebraic expressions and solve linear equations
Use mathematical models to represent and understand quantitative relationships	• model and solve contextualized problems using various representations, such as graphs, tables, and equations.
Analyze change in various contexts	• use graphs to analyze the nature of changes in quantities in linear relationships.

Fig. 1.51. Algebra Standard and Expectations for grades 6–8 from *Principles and Standards for School Mathematics* (NCTM 2000, p. 222)

have their basis in many of the ideas that we have developed in this chapter. For instance, the grade 6 standard related to expressions and equations (6.EE) calls for students to be able to do the following:

- Apply and extend previous understandings of arithmetic to algebraic expressions
- Reason about and solve one-variable equations and inequalities
- Represent and analyze quantitative relationships between dependent and independent variables. (CCSSI 2010, pp. 43–44)

In our discussion of Big Idea 1 (Expressions) and Big Idea 2 (Variables), we explored ideas related to the first element, which calls for a transfer of understanding from arithmetic to algebra. Our elaboration of Big Idea 3 (Equality) and Big Idea 5 (Solving equa-

Big Idea 2

Variables.
Variables are tools for expressing mathematical ideas clearly and concisely. They have many different meanings, depending on context and purpose.

tions) fleshed out the reasoning described in the second element, and our treatment of Big Idea 4 (Representing and analyzing functions) addressed the skills outlined in the third element.

As a final example from the Common Core State Standards, consider the grade 8 standard related to functions (8.F), which calls for students to know how to do the following:

- Define, evaluate, and compare functions
- Use functions to model relationships between quantities (CCSSI 2010, p. 55)

The essential understandings associated with Big Idea 4 (Representing and analyzing functions) provide an extensive basis for instruction in support of this standard. Our hope is that when teachers are equipped with a deep understanding of algebra, they will be well positioned to help students learn important mathematics in meaningful ways.

Big Idea 3

Equality. *The equals sign indicates that two expressions are equivalent. It can also be used in defining or naming a single expression or function rule.*

Big Idea 4

Representing and analyzing functions. *Functions provide a means for describing and understanding relationships between variables. They can have multiple representations—in algebraic symbols, situations, graphs, verbal descriptions, tables, and so on—and they can be classified into different* families *with similar patterns of change.*

Big Idea 5

Solving equations. *General algorithms exist for solving many kinds of equations; these algorithms are broadly applicable for solving a wide range of similar equations. However, for some problems or situations, alternatives to these general algorithms may be more elegant, efficient, or informative.*

Chapter

2

Connections: Looking Back and Ahead in Learning

In chapter 1, we explored five big ideas related to teachers' understanding of expressions, equations, and functions at the middle school level. These areas of algebra are also important elements of students' learning in the upper elementary grades and high school. How do the big ideas that we have developed connect to mathematics that students encounter before and after middle school? A response to this question is the focus of chapter 2.

Connections in Grades 3–5

In grades 3–5, students work with general properties of addition and multiplication. They begin to use variables to represent numbers in statements of commutativity and associativity as well as to stand for quantities in story problems. They explore a variety of patterns and develop rudimentary ideas about functions. This work lays a strong foundation for the ideas about expressions, equations, and functions that students encounter in grades 6–8.

General properties of addition and multiplication

In grades 3–5, students develop and use properties of addition and multiplication of real numbers, including the associative and commutative properties, identity and inverse properties, and the distributive property of multiplication over addition. Students also develop understandings of addition and subtraction, and multiplication and division, as inverse relationships. When teachers help students in grades 3–5 to develop an understanding of general properties of arithmetic, they are also preparing students to apply those properties later to generate equivalent expressions, as we explored in our discussion of symbolic transformations that preserve the equivalence of expressions on both sides of an equals sign (Essential Understanding 1c).

Essential Understanding 1c
A relatively small number of symbolic transformations can be applied to expressions to yield equivalent expressions.

Students can gain insight into the meaning of multiplication by connecting it with the idea of the area of a rectangle and working with area models of multiplication. For example, they might be taught that 4×5 can be represented with a rectangle with side lengths of 4 and 5. Teachers recognize that this representation is helpful for illustrating some other properties of multiplication.

In the elementary grades, teachers often ask students to use the distributive property to compose and decompose numbers in ways that allow the students to solve problems with understanding. For instance, to calculate the value of 5×23, students discover that it makes sense to multiply 5×20 and 5×3 and add these partial products:

$$5 \times 23 = 5 \times (20 + 3) = (5 \times 20) + (5 \times 3)$$

In figure 2.1, the purple area represents 5×20. There are 5 rows of 20 purple squares. The gray area represents 5×3 with 5 rows of 3 gray squares. The large rectangle consists of 5 rows of 23 squares and represents the product 5×23.

For a longer discussion of models and properties of multiplication, see *Developing Essential Understanding of Multiplication and Division for Teaching Mathematics in Grades 3–5* (Otto et al. 2011).

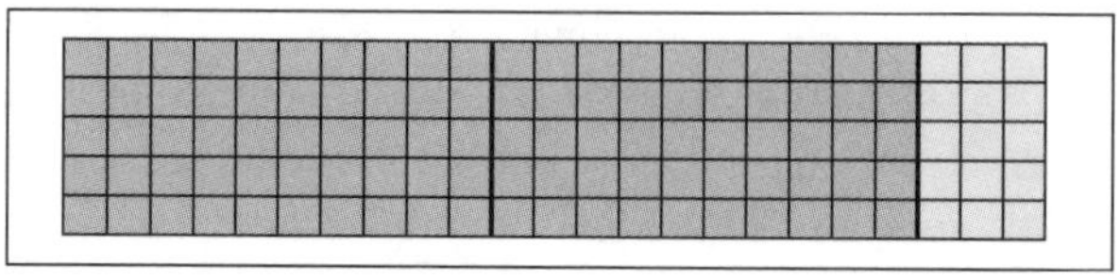

Fig. 2.1. A representation of 5×23 as $(5 \times 20) + (5 \times 3)$

This same property—the distributive property of multiplication over addition for real numbers—allows us to reason about equivalent algebraic expressions. For example, an area model of multiplication, like the one used above, can help us "see" that $3(3x + 2)$ and $9x + 6$ are equivalent expressions. In figure 2.2, the purple area represents the product $3 \times 3x$, and the gray area represents 3×2.

$$3(3x + 2) = 3 \times 3x + 3 \times 2 = 9x + 6$$

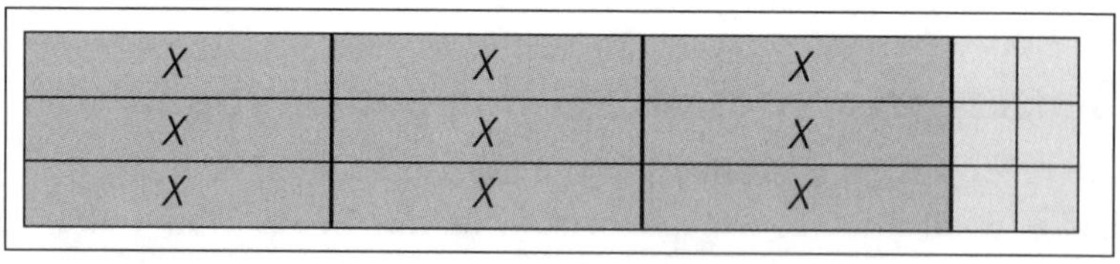

Fig. 2.2. A representation of $3(3x + 2)$ as $3 \times 3x + 3 \times 2$

Essential Understanding 1c *A relatively small number of symbolic transformations can be applied to expressions to yield equivalent expressions.*

Understanding the distributive property can help us in both "putting together" and "taking apart" expressions to find equivalent expressions (Essential Understanding 1c). Figure 2.2 illustrates both putting together (or composing, in this case by multiplying) the factors 3 and $3x + 2$ to obtain the expression $9x + 6$, and taking apart (or decomposing, by factoring) $9x + 6$ into the factors 3 and $3x + 2$.

As teachers in the elementary grades engage students in working with more sophisticated multiplication and division problems and strategies, they continue to help their students build a foundation for future work with expressions involving variables. For example, students in grades 3–5 come to understand that to calculate the value of 25 × 23, it is insufficient to add 20 × 20 and 5 × 3. Additional partial products are involved—namely, 5 × 20 and 20 × 3, the light purple and darker purple regions, respectively, of the rectangle in figure 2.3. As we discussed in connection with Essential Understanding 1c, this understanding provides the basis for analyzing and determining the equivalence of algebraic expressions. Reflect 2.1 invites you to consider how the multiplication of two linear expressions is related to the product represented in figure 2.3.

An extended discussion of properties of number and operations as a basis for developing algebraic ideas appears in *Developing Essential Understanding of Algebraic Thinking for Teaching Mathematics in Grades 3–5* (Blanton et al. 2011).

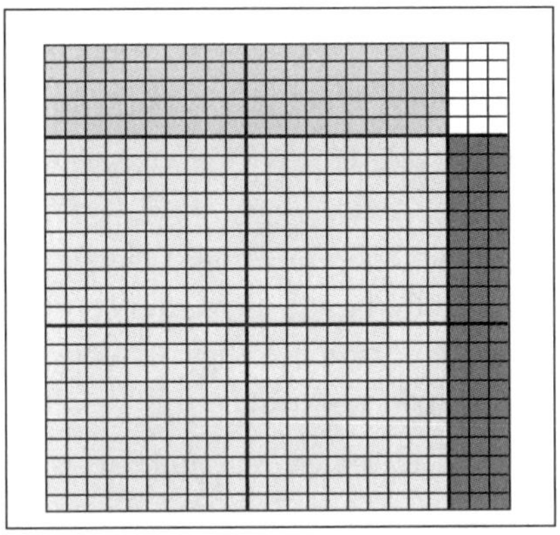

Fig. 2.3. An illustration of the partial products for 25 × 23

Reflect 2.1

How might you use algebra tiles and an area model to determine whether $(x + 3)(3x + 2)$ and $3x^2 + 6$ are equivalent expressions? How does your understanding of the distributive property, and other general properties, come into play as you consider this question?

Figure 2.4 shows a rectangle with height $x + 3$ and width $3x + 2$, constructed by using algebra tiles. The area of this rectangle is $(x + 3)(3x + 2)$, which is equivalent to $3x^2 + 11x + 6$, as shown in the figure. So, $(x + 3)(3x + 2)$ and $3x^2 + 6$ are not equivalent expressions. A representation like the one in the figure can be helpful for encouraging students to develop understanding of their work in algebra.

Variables, expressions, and equations

When we view the properties of addition and multiplication discussed above as general properties that work for all real numbers, we encounter *variables*. Letters are customarily used to represent

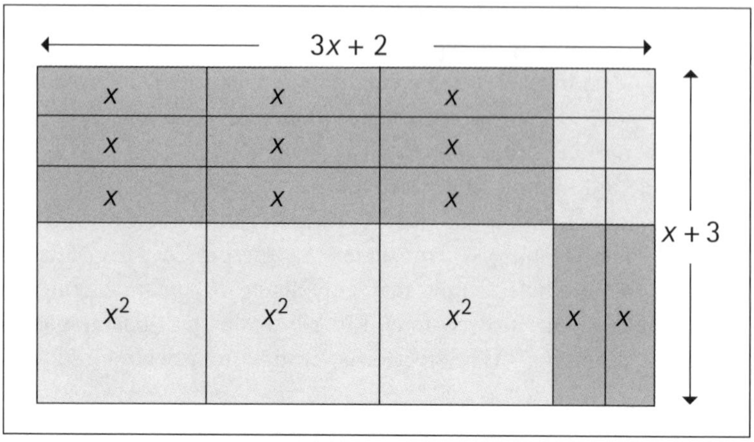

Fig. 2.4. Algebra tiles illustrating $(x + 3)(3x + 2)$ is not equivalent to $3x^2 + 6$

real numbers in these general properties. Developing an understanding of these properties often gives elementary students their first exposure to variables. For example, the commutative property of addition can be expressed as follows:

$$a + b = b + a, \text{ for any real numbers } a \text{ and } b.$$

Students in grades 3–5 gain further experiences with variables as they represent and solve story problems and describe patterns in terms of symbolic expressions and equations. Consider the following situation:

> The service club is planning a soccer game (Maroon Team versus Gray Team) to raise money. The students plan to charge $2 per ticket for entry to the game. If a group of friends spends $14 on tickets, how many tickets did they purchase?

A student might use the variable n to describe the cost of buying n tickets with the expression $2 \times n$. The student can then write an equation representing the equivalence of the quantity 14 and the quantity $2 \times n$ as $14 = 2 \times n$. Another student might write the following equation: $14/n = 2$. It is important for the teacher to recognize that these equations are equivalent (assuming that the friends purchased at least one ticket and n is not equal to 0) and to understand why they are equivalent.

In both of these equations, the variable n represents an unknown quantity of tickets. Symbolically, solving either equation demands that students have an understanding of the inverse relationship between multiplication and division, a key idea in the elementary mathematics curriculum. In the examples, variables are used in different ways, to express different things. The need for teachers to help students navigate among these different uses of variable underscores the importance of Essential Understanding 2*a*.

As the big ideas emphasize, expressions and equations are powerful tools for representing and analyzing relationships. To analyze the soccer game situation described above, it is helpful to develop a general rule that relates the variables. If the service club members are thinking about how much income ticket sales will generate, they might develop the following equation:

$I = 2 \times n$, where I represents income and n represents tickets sold.

This equation describes a proportional relationship between two variables.

Over time, as students in grades 6–8 become increasingly comfortable in using mathematical notation to represent their thinking, teachers can encourage them to explore more complex relationships between variables. For instance, suppose the club has \$500 worth of expenses for the soccer game. If n represents the number of tickets sold, and P represents the profit for the club, the students can describe the relationship between n and P in the following equation:

$$P = 2 \times n - 500$$

Thinking about the two variables, n and P, as related in this way can help students to recognize that the service club would need to sell 250 tickets to break even. This break-even point can be seen on the graph in figure 2.5 as the point at which the profit line crosses the horizontal axis (when $P = 0$). In the table of values that the figure also shows, the break-even point appears in the row in

Essential Understanding 2*a*
Variables have many different meanings, depending on context and purpose.

For a discussion of the inverse relationship between multiplication and division, see *Developing Essential Understanding of Multiplication and Division for Teaching Mathematics in Grades 3–5* (Otto et al. 2011).

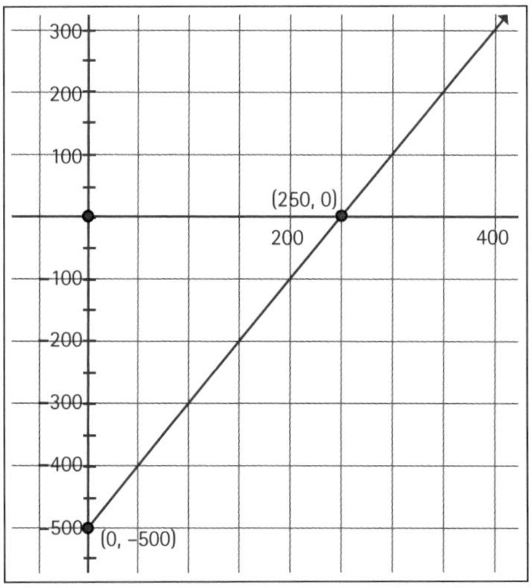

Number of tickets sold (n)	Profit (P)
0	-500
50	-400
100	-300
150	-200
200	-100
250	0
300	100
350	200
400	300

Fig. 2.5. A graph and a table of values representing profit from a soccer game for which organizers sell tickets for \$2 each and have \$500 of expenses

which profit is zero and the number of tickets sold is 250. This more complex relationship, which might be examined by students in the upper elementary grades, is very similar to the profit situation that you explored in Reflect 1.21 and we then discussed in depth.

Patterns and functions

In the elementary grades, students explore a variety of patterns and represent them in words, tables, graphs, and symbols. It is important for teachers to understand the role that multiple representations play in analyses of patterns of change. This use of different representations is expressed in Essential Understanding 4*b*. Middle school teachers who have developed this understanding can appreciate the value of the work that elementary school students do in making predictions about what comes next in a pattern or sequence and developing generalizations about relationships in patterns. Consider the growing pattern in figure 2.6.

➔ Essential Understanding 4*b*
Functions can be represented in multiple ways—in algebraic symbols, situations, graphs, verbal descriptions, tables, and so on—and these representations, and the links among them, are useful in analyzing patterns of change.

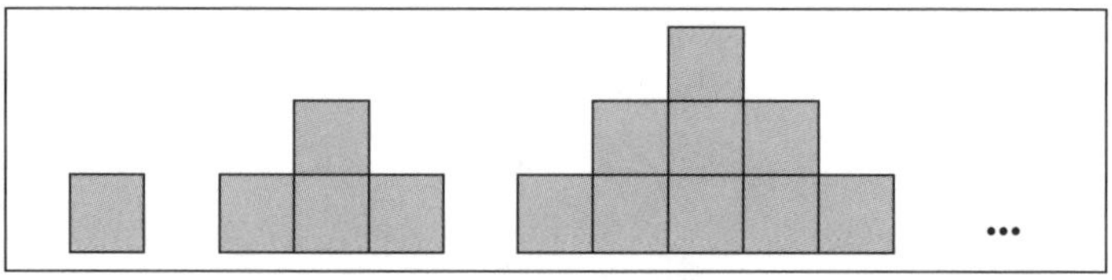

Fig. 2.6. A pattern of tiles

Students in grades 3–5 might make sense of and figure out how to continue the pattern by drawing or arranging tiles. They are able to describe this pattern with words and numbers. Students might describe the shapes as being made up of a number of unit squares that are sums of consecutive odd numbers: 1 square, 1 + 3 squares, and 1 + 3 + 5 squares. Recognition of the pattern allows students to identify the next element in the pattern, a shape made up of 1 + 3 + 5 + 7 squares. Some students in grades 3–5 recognize that by counting the number of unit squares that compose the shape, they are determining the area of the shape. Reflect 2.2 encourages you to investigate *area* in this pattern.

Reflect 2.2

Represent the relationship between a shape's position in the pattern in figure 2.6 and its area by using a table, graph, and equation. Think about what essential understandings you are drawing on as you consider this pattern.

We can use a table such as that in figure 2.7 to represent the relationship between the shape's position in the pattern and its area. This table draws attention to the idea that the pattern suggests a squaring function. If n represents the position in the pattern, then the area for that position is n^2. (You may have noticed that the unit squares that compose each shape can be rearranged to form a square.)

Position in the pattern	Area of the shape in that position (square units)
1	1
2	4
3	9
4	16
5	25
6	36

Fig. 2.7. A table of values representing the areas of shapes in the pattern in fig. 2.6

Different representations of the pattern of change in this situation are related to Essential Understanding 4*b*. These representations are useful for analyzing the nature of the rate of change in this relationship. By generating a graph on a graphing calculator, we can see that the rate of change in this relationship is nonlinear. By examining the table, we can see that the rate of change is changing at a constant rate. The first differences are +3, +5, +7, +9, ... , and the second differences are constant (+2). Constant second differences are characteristic of quadratic relationships, as we explored in our discussion of Essential Understanding 4*f*. Although students in grades 3–5 are unlikely to explore first and second differences, they are likely to identify and articulate qualities of this pattern of change—for example that the areas increase more and more quickly as the sequence progresses.

Essential Understanding 4*b* *Functions can be represented in multiple ways—in algebraic symbols, situations, graphs, verbal descriptions, tables, and so on—and these representations, and the links among them, are useful in analyzing patterns of change.*

Essential Understanding 4*f* *Quadratic functions are characterized by rates of change that change at a constant rate.*

The pattern of change in this quadratic relationship becomes more apparent if we contrast it with the pattern of change in another relationship. Let's consider the relationship between a shape's position in the pattern in figure 2.6 and its *perimeter*. A table of values is shown in figure 2.8.

As we move from one term in the pattern to the next, the perimeter of the shape increases by 6. In contrast to the quadratic relationship of Reflect 2.2, this relationship has a constant rate of change and is linear. The constant rate of change is also visible in a graph of this relationship (see fig. 2.9). Students in the elementary grades will recognize that the points (position, perimeter) fall on a line.

Teachers who possess the essential understandings related to Big Idea 4 (Representing and analyzing functions) can see the value of experiences that students have had in grades 3–5 and can help students build on those experiences in grades 6–8. When elementary students develop and compare graphs, tables, symbolic rules,

Big Idea 4

Functions provide a means for describing and understanding relationships between variables. They can have multiple representations—in algebraic symbols, situations, graphs, verbal descriptions, tables, and so on—and they can be classified into different families with similar patterns of change.

Position in the pattern	Perimeter of the shape in that position (linear units)
1	4
2	10
3	16
4	22
5	28
6	34

Fig. 2.8. A table of values representing the perimeters of shapes in the pattern in fig. 2.6

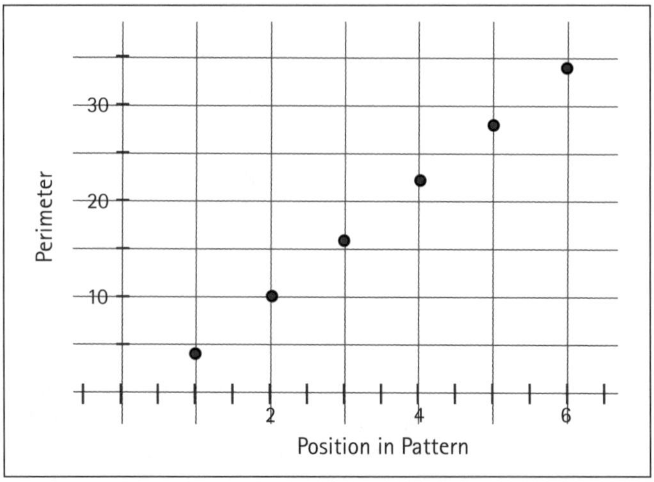

Fig. 2.9. A graph representing the perimeters of shapes in the pattern in fig. 2.6

and verbal descriptions for different relationships emerging from the same pattern, as we have done in the example of the pattern in figure 2.6, they have opportunities to express and generalize relationships. They are also able to begin to recognize and understand the characteristic patterns of change for linear and nonlinear functions that their mathematics experiences in middle school and high school mathematics will develop further.

Connections in Grades 9–12

The understanding of expressions, equations, and functions that students gain in grades 6–8 leads directly to some of the most important work of high school mathematics—developing a robust understanding of functions and solving increasingly complex equations. The emerging awareness that students gain in grades 6–8 of families of functions prepares them to encounter other function families in high school and use their characteristics in solving problems and modeling real-world situations.

Functions

Functions are one of the most important topics in the high school mathematics curriculum. In grades 9–12, students encounter a wider variety of functions and extend their appreciation for both the complexity and the power of functions. Whereas middle school students most commonly work with linear, quadratic, and exponential functions, high school students encounter a curriculum that includes in-depth exploration of these types of functions, as well as other families of polynomial functions, logarithmic functions, trigonometric functions, rational functions, and inverse functions.

Essential Understanding 4*b*
Functions can be represented in multiple ways—in algebraic symbols, situations, graphs, verbal descriptions, tables, and so on—and these representations, and the links among them, are useful in analyzing patterns of change.

High school students' understanding of function families continues to build on exploration of multiple representations: words, graphs, tables, and symbols. As our exploration of Essential Understanding 4*b* indicated, these representations provide valuable information about different patterns of change in relationships. At the high school level, teachers continue to engage students in using multiple representations to develop their understanding of a variety of function relationships. It is valuable for teachers of mathematics in grades 6–8 to be aware of how their students' understanding will continue to develop in high school mathematics courses.

For example, explorations of quadratic functions in grades 9–12 examine alternatives to the standard form, $f(x) = ax^2 + bx + c$, and what these alternatives illuminate about the behavior of quadratic functions. In particular, students in grades 9–12 discover that all quadratic functions can also be written in *vertex form:* $f(x) = a(x - h)^2 + k$, where a, h, and k are constants and a is not equal to 0. Vertex form has the advantage of providing some useful information about the graph of a quadratic function. The constant a in the vertex form can tell us if the graph of a quadratic function, a parabola, has a maximum or a minimum point (in other words, whether the graph opens up or down). If $a > 0$, then the point (h, k) is a minimum. If $a < 0$, then the point (h, k) is a maximum. In both cases, the point (h, k) is a *vertex.*

When a quadratic function is expressed in the vertex form $f(x)= a(x - h)^2 + k$, we can also obtain information about the x-intercepts of the graph, if any such intercepts exist. The x-intercepts are associated with the quadratic function's *zeros*, or the x-values for which the quadratic function has a value of 0. So, to find the x-intercepts, or to conclude that none exist, we can solve the equation $a(x - h)^2 + k = 0$. The following equations are equivalent if an x-intercept exists:

$$a(x - h)^2 + k = 0$$

$$(x - h)^2 = \frac{-k}{a}$$

$$x - h = \pm\sqrt{\frac{-k}{a}}$$

$$x = h \pm \sqrt{\frac{-k}{a}}$$

So, the x-intercepts, if they exist, occur at

$$x = h \pm \sqrt{\frac{-k}{a}},$$

symmetrically about the vertical line that contains the vertex (h, k). The number of x-intercepts depends on the value of $-k/a$. There is one x-intercept if $-k/a = 0$, and thus $\sqrt{-k/a} = 0$, and no x-intercept if $-k/a$ is negative. Weeks (2003) provides an extended graphical connection to complex solutions of quadratic equations. Consider the contextual example in Reflect 2.3 to appreciate the usefulness of the vertex form.

Reflect 2.3

Imagine that a 6-foot-tall soccer player heads a ball at a vertical velocity of 16 feet per second. The height of the ball (in feet) x seconds later can be described by the quadratic function $f(x) =-16x^2 + 16x + 6$. What is the maximum height that the soccer ball reaches? How much time elapses from the instant when the ball was hit until the instant when it hits the ground?

➜ Essential Understanding 5c *Quadratic equations can be solved by using graphs and tables and by applying an algorithm that involves* completing the square. *This algorithm, when expressed in a more compact form, is also known as the* quadratic formula.

It is possible to find approximate values for these points by using tables and graphs, as students at the middle school level commonly would. However, if we can express the function in vertex form, then we can also use symbolic methods to find the exact zeros and the vertex of the quadratic. To rewrite $f(x) = -16x^2 + 16x + 6$ in the vertex form $y = a(x - h)^2 + k$, we can "complete the square" (using the process that we demonstrated in our discussion of Essential Understanding 5c). This algorithm transforms an equation from the standard form ($y = ax^2 + bx + c$) into a perfect square form like the one that appears in the vertex form.

Completing the square for the function in Reflect 2.3 yields $f(x)= -16(x - 1/2)^2 + 10$. From this equation in vertex form, we can conclude that the maximum height of the soccer ball is 10 feet and that it reaches this height 0.5 seconds after the player heads it. We can also use the vertex form to determine when the ball hits the ground. The ball will hit the ground when $f(x) = 0$, so we need to solve the equation $-16(x - 1/2)^2 + 10 = 0$. To solve this equation, we can proceed through the following equivalent equations:

$$-16\left(x-\frac{1}{2}\right)^2+10=0$$

$$\left(x-\frac{1}{2}\right)^2=\frac{5}{8}$$

$$x-\frac{1}{2}=\pm\sqrt{\frac{5}{8}}$$

$$x=\frac{1}{2}\pm\sqrt{\frac{5}{8}}$$

The soccer ball hits the ground approximately 1.29 seconds after it is headed. (In this context, $x \approx -0.29$ seconds does not make sense, because the ball cannot hit the ground before it is headed!)

Notice that by drawing on the vertex form, we obtain a good deal of information that we can use to create a rough sketch of the graph of this relationship. We know that (0.5, 10) is the maximum point on the graph and that the x-intercepts are

$$\left(\frac{1}{2}-\sqrt{\frac{5}{8}},\ 0\right) \quad \text{and} \quad \left(\frac{1}{2}+\sqrt{\frac{5}{8}},\ 0\right).$$

The graph of the height of the soccer ball over time is shown in figure 2.10.

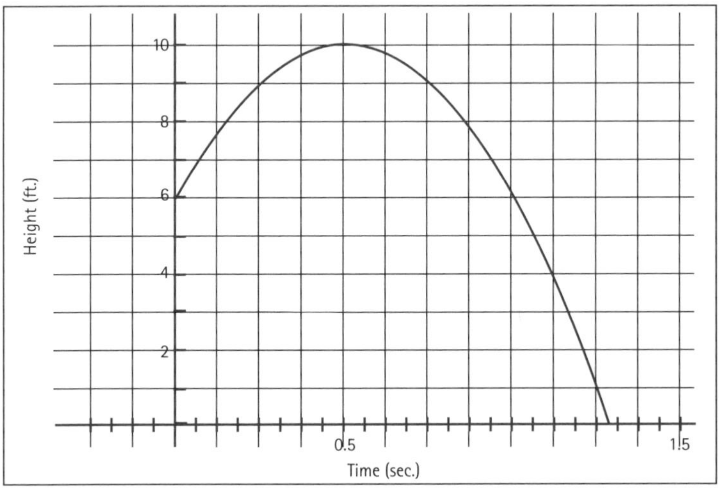

Fig. 2.10. The graph that describes the height of a soccer ball (in feet) x seconds after it is headed and until it hits the ground is a portion of the graph of the quadratic function $f(x) = -16x^2 + 16x + 6$.

As illustrated in the examples above, as well as in the examples that we considered in our discussion of Big Idea 4, multiple representations and links among them are very useful for analyzing functions (Essential Understanding 4*b*). When we examined linear

Big Idea 4

Functions provide a means for describing and understanding relationships between variables. They can have multiple representations—in algebraic symbols, situations, graphs, verbal descriptions, tables, and so on—and they can be classified into different families *with similar patterns of change.*

Essential Understanding 4*b*
Functions can be represented in multiple ways—in algebraic symbols, situations, graphs, verbal descriptions, tables, and so on—and these representations, and the links among them, are useful in analyzing patterns of change.

functions, we illustrated the particular value of building connections between symbolic and graphical representations (see Reflects 1.24, 1.25, and 1.26). Many of the essential understandings that we developed in connection with Big Idea 4 can provide the basis for similar analysis of quadratic functions and other families of functions–analysis that is common in grades 9–12. For example, if we are given a rule for a quadratic function, it can be helpful to recognize how its graph relates to the graph of the basic parabola for $f(x) = x^2$. This is the focus of Reflect 2.4.

Reflect 2.4

What can you say about the graph of each function described below, on the basis of what you know about the graph of $q(x) = x^2$?

$P_1(x) = x^2 + 3$ $\quad P_2(x) = 2x^2$ $\quad P_3(x) = \frac{1}{4}x^2$ $\quad P_4(x) = -\frac{1}{4}x^2$

As illustrated in figure 2.11, the graph corresponding to $q(x)$ is a parabola with minimum point at the origin (0, 0). The graph corresponding to $P_1(x)$ has the same shape as that corresponding to $q(x)$ but is shifted vertically 3 units in the positive (upward) direction. This translating effect on the graph of adding a constant to the function expression is the same effect that we observed in the case of linear functions (see, for example, Reflect 1.26).

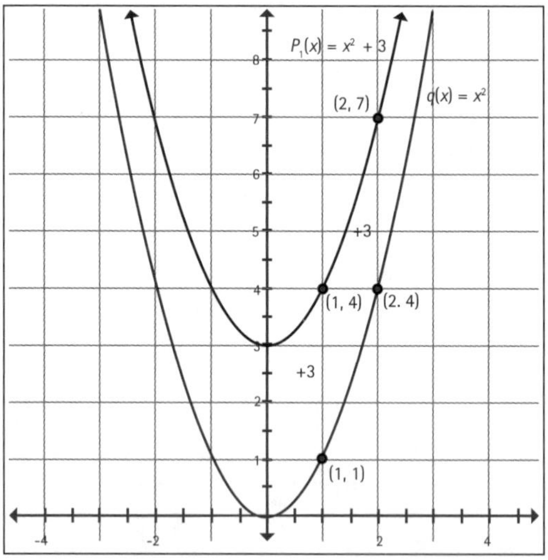

Fig. 2.11. The graph of $P_1(x)$ has the same shape as that of $q(x)$ but is shifted vertically 3 units in the positive (upward) direction.

Figure 2.12 shows how the graph corresponding to $P_2(x) = 2x^2$ opens upward and has its minimum point at the origin, as does the graph of $q(x)$. Although the parabola corresponding to $P_2(x)$ might appear to be narrower than the parabola corresponding to $q(x)$, it is actually a vertically scaled version of the graph of $q(x)$. For every nonzero input, the output of P_2 will be twice the output of q. This relationship can be seen in a table of values for these functions (see fig. 2.13). For example, $q(1) = 1$, but $P_2(1) = 2$. The points (1, 1) on the graph of q and (1, 2) on the graph of P_2 are shown in figure 2.12.

For additional detail about the rescaling of axes that results when the function $q(x) = x^2$ is multiplied by a constant function with a positive constant, see *Developing Essential Understanding of Functions for Teaching Mathematics in Grades 9–12* (Cooney, Beckmann, and Lloyd 2010, pp. 71–72).

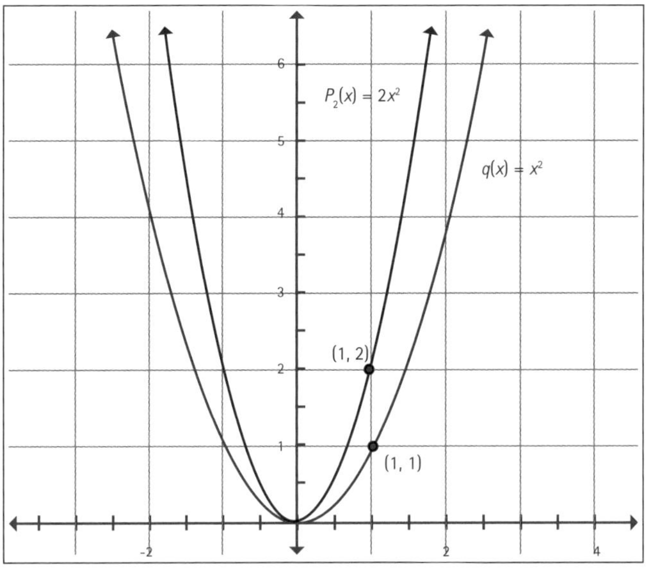

Fig. 2.12. The graph corresponding to $P_2(x)$ is a parabola that has the origin as its minimum point and is a vertically scaled version of the parabola corresponding to $q(x)$.

Like the graphs corresponding to q and P_2, the graph corresponding to P_3 opens upward and has its minimum point at the origin. However, as shown in figure 2.14, the parabola corresponding to $P_3(x)$ is a different vertically scaled version of the parabola corresponding to $q(x)$. We can see from the table in figure 2.13 that for every nonzero input, the output of P_3 is one-fourth the output of q. For example, $q(2) = 4$, but $P_3(2) = 1$. The points (2, 4) on the graph of q and (2, 1) on the graph of P_3 are shown in figure 2.14.

The graph corresponding to $P_4(x) = -1/4\,x^2$, shown in figure 2.14, has exactly the same shape as that corresponding to $P_3(x) = 1/4x^2$; however, it is reflected across the x-axis. As shown in the table in figure 2.13, for any x, $P_4(x) =-P_3(x)$. This is consistent with the results that we discussed in connection with the explorations of linear functions in Reflect 1.25 and 1.26.

In our discussion of Big Idea 4, we observed that for a linear function, adding a constant to a function expression results in a vertical translation of the graph of the function and that multiplying by a constant affects the slope of the graph. In Reflect 2.4, you extended the analysis to quadratic functions and observed that a similar vertical translation in the graph of $q(x) = x^2$ results from

Big Idea 4

Functions provide a means for describing and understanding relationships between variables. They can have multiple representations—in algebraic symbols, situations, graphs, verbal descriptions, tables, and so on—and they can be classified into different families *with similar* patterns of change.

x	$q(x) = x^2$	$P_1(x) = x^2 + 3$	$P_2(x) = 2x^2$	$P_3(x) = \frac{1}{4}x^2$	$P_4(x) = -\frac{1}{4}x^2$
-3	9	12	18	$\frac{9}{4}$	$-\frac{9}{4}$
-2	4	7	8	1	-1
-1	1	4	2	$-\frac{1}{4}$	$-\frac{1}{4}$
0	0	3	0	0	0
1	1	4	2	$\frac{1}{4}$	$-\frac{1}{4}$
2	4	7	8	1	-1
3	9	12	18	$\frac{9}{4}$	$-\frac{9}{4}$

Fig. 2.13. A table of values for functions built from $q(x) = x^2$

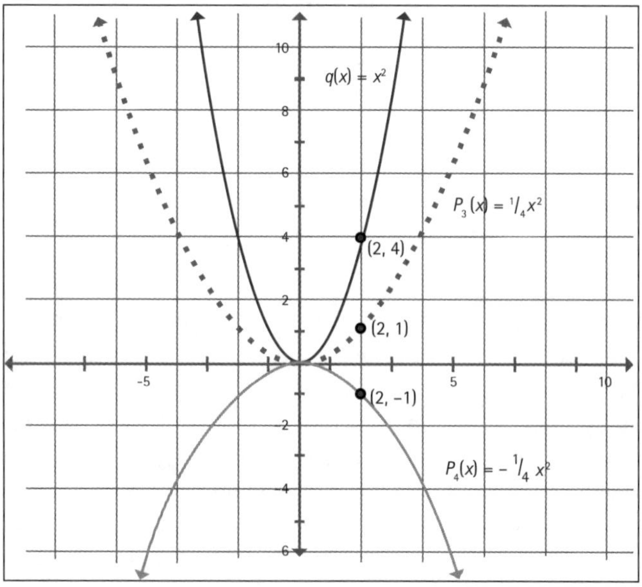

Fig. 2.14. The graph of P_4 is the same as the graph of P_3 but is reflected across the x-axis.

adding a constant, and a vertical scaling (as well as possibly a reflection across the x-axis) results from multiplying by a constant. These patterns in geometric transformations of graphs illustrate how explorations of multiple representations of linear functions in grades 6–8 can provide a foundation for further experiences with quadratic functions, and other families of functions, in grades 9–12.

For another illustration of how the concepts that we explored in connection with Big Idea 4 provide the basis for the treatment of functions in high school, let's turn briefly to exponential functions. In general, exponential relationships can be described by expressions of the form $a \cdot b^x$ where $b > 0$. In the relationship $y = a \cdot b^x$, b is the "base" that determines the rate of increase or decrease, and a is the y-intercept of the graph and sometimes called the "starting point" in applied situations.

For example, in Reflect 1.30, you investigated the pattern of change in the growth of a plant and tried to develop a recursive way to express that growth. We then analyzed the function $g(t) = 10 \cdot 2^t$ as another way to represent the height of the plant over time. When we use this exponential function to model the plant's growth, our starting point is 10 millimeters (the initial height of the plant), and the base of the function, 2, is the factor by which the plant's height increases each week.

In Reflect 1.31, you examined the use of another exponential function $k(t) = 32 \cdot (1/2)^t$ to model the number of teams that remain in an elimination soccer tournament after t rounds. When we use the function $k(t)$ to model the tournament situation, we have a different starting point and a different base from the ones that we have when we use the function $g(t)$ to model the situation of the plant's growth. How do the graphs of these functions compare? Revisit figures 1.40 and 1.42 to consider this question. Then turn to Reflect 2.5 to think more generally about how different values of b for the base affect an exponential relationship.

Reflect 2.5

Experiment with different values of $b > 0$ in relationships of the form $y = a \cdot b^x$. You may want to work with relationships in which $a = 1$ (in other words, those of the form $y = b^x$), so that you can focus on the role of b. Note that if $b = 1$, the relationship $y = a \cdot b^x$ can be rewritten as $y = a$, a constant relationship.

When the base is greater than 1, as in the function $g(t)$ that we used to model the plant's height over time, the relationship is increasing. As t increases, $g(t)$ increases. The larger the base, the faster the rate of growth. So, for example, the graph corresponding to a plant's growth that can be described by the equation $j(t) = 10 \cdot 3^t$ will increase more quickly than the graph of $g(t)$ (shown in figure 1.40).

If the base of an exponential relationship is between 0 and 1, as in the example of $k(t)$, the relationship is decreasing. The smaller the base, the faster the rate of decrease. For example, if we compare $y = (2/3)^x$ and $y = (1/5)^x$, we will find that $y = (2/3)^x$ decreases more slowly than $y = (1/5)^x$. Figure 2.15 shows that the graph of $y = (2/3)^x$ decreases more slowly than the graph of $y = (1/5)^x$.

We have now considered examples of the way that analysis of functions in grades 9–12 builds on understanding developed in

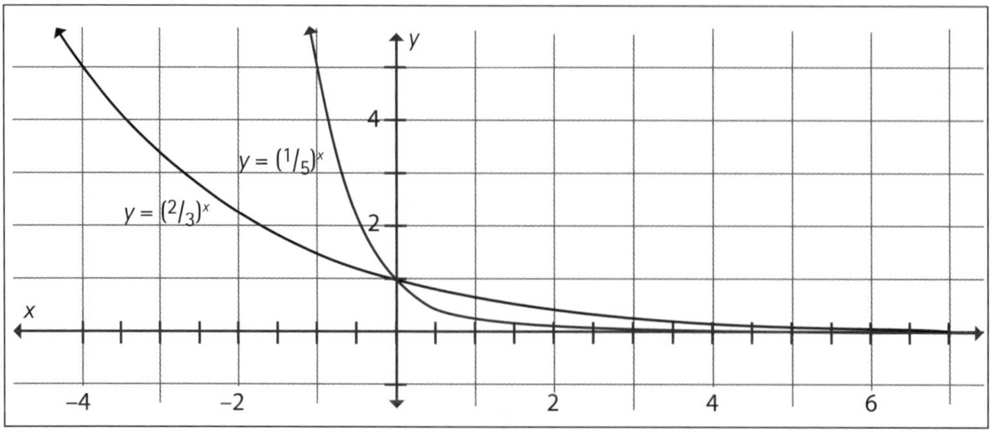

Fig. 2.15. Comparing the graphs corresponding to $y = (2/3)^x$ and $y = (1/5)^x$

For a discussion of functions for which domain and range are not sets of numbers, see *Developing Essential Understanding of Functions for Teaching Mathematics in Grades 9–12* (Cooney, Beckmann, and Lloyd 2010).

grades 6–8 and relates to ideas that we explored in chapter 1. In addition to gaining further experience with linear, quadratic, and exponential functions, high school students work with new families of functions, including other families of polynomial functions, logarithmic functions, trigonometric functions, rational functions, and inverse functions. When high school students encounter these new families of functions, they bring with them their earlier experiences in which they analyzed relationships between variables and represented relationships in multiple ways. Although most functions that students explore in the middle grades are described by algebraic expressions, it is important for teachers to know that functions do not always follow "rules" and cannot always be described by algebraic expressions. The domain and range of a function do not even need to be numbers!

Solving equations

As part of exploring a broader variety of functions, students in grades 9–12 also need to find solutions to many different kinds of equations. As with linear and quadratic equations such as those that we explored in chapter 1, all equations that students face can be solved by using a variety of representations, including graphs, tables, and symbols. Some of the techniques used for solving linear and quadratic equations are quite useful for solving more complex equations, but in other instances new transformations are needed.

For example, consider exponential equations such as one that we explored in chapter 1 as a model for plant B's growth: $g(t) = 10 \cdot 2^t$. Our discussion of figures 1.39 and 1.40 illustrated how graphs and tables can be useful in solving exponential equations. Reflect 2.6 offers an opportunity to think about symbolic methods for solving exponential equations.

Reflect 2.6

What symbolic methods have you taught your students for solving exponential equations? Do you know whether an algorithm exists for solving exponential equations, just as algorithms exist for solving linear and quadratic equations?

To answer the question in Reflect 2.6, let's consider the exponential function that described the growth of plant B, $g(t) = 10 \cdot 2^t$. If we are interested in determining how many weeks it would take for plant B to grow to a height of 100 inches, we can write the exponential equation:

$$10 \cdot 2^t = 100$$

As with other types of equations, our goal in solving this equation is to find the value of t that makes the two expressions $10 \cdot 2^t$ and 100 have the same value. Many of the symbolic transformations previously identified as useful for solving linear and quadratic equations are also useful in solving exponential equations. In this example, if we multiply both expressions by $1/10$ (by the multiplication property of equality), we transform the equation to an equivalent one:

$$2^t = 10$$

From here, a symbolic transformation that is useful for solving exponential equations is taking the logarithm of both sides:

$$\log(2^t) = \log(10)$$

The laws of logarithms provide a set of symbolic transformations that preserve the equivalence of two expressions; using such laws, we can rewrite this equation as

$$t \log(2) = 1,$$

which means that $t = 1/\log(2)$.

The more general observation is that as teachers expand the types and complexity of equations that students work with in grades 9–12, they also expand their students' repertoires of symbolic transformations that ensure the equivalence of expressions on both sides of an equals sign, allowing the students to work with increasingly challenging equations. Fundamentally, the process of symbolically solving an equation is the same, regardless of the complexity of the equation. We apply symbolic transformations that ensure the equivalence of two expressions so that we can find the value(s) of the variable that yield the same value for the two expressions. Sometimes algorithms can be applied to solve equations, but more generally (as discussed in relation to Big Idea 5) it is important for teachers to help students make strategic decisions in the selection of transformations to use to arrive at solutions (if they exist) in ways that are efficient and elegant.

Big Idea 5

General algorithms exist for solving many kinds of equations; these algorithms are broadly applicable for solving a wide range of similar equations. However, for some problems or situations, alternatives to these general algorithms may be more elegant, efficient, or informative.

Conclusion

This chapter has described some of the roles that the five big ideas about expressions, equations, and functions play in students' learning in the elementary and high school grades. Understanding the typical mathematical experiences of students, both before and after their time in your classroom, can strengthen your grasp of the big ideas and essential understandings and help you to support students' learning of algebra in the middle grades.

Chapter 3

Challenges: Learning, Teaching, and Assessing

In this chapter, we discuss challenges that students encounter in learning about expressions, equations, and functions, as well as some implications of these challenges for instruction and assessment. To do so, we draw on research about the teaching and learning of algebra.

Expressions

Algebra is often one of the first areas of school mathematics in which students are asked to solve problems that do not necessarily produce a single-term answer. Yet, the sense of "closure" that producing such answers brings (Tabach and Friedlander 2008) occurs almost exclusively when students study operations with whole numbers, integers, and rational numbers. In this case, by *closure*, we mean that students consider their work on a mathematics problem to be finished because they obtain a single number or quantity for their answer. In some ways, using expressions to represent a number or quantity redefines what mathematics is for students because the focus might now be on representing a *process*. For example, an answer to a problem in algebra might be $5x + 2$, which students might interpret as a lack of closure. Sometimes students might reduce this expression to 7 or $7x$ because their previous experiences have taught them that an answer to a mathematics problem should consist of a single term or number. Though students might feel compelled to combine terms, it is not always appropriate for them to do so. Reflect 3.1 encourages you to explore ways of handling students' perplexity on this point.

Reflect 3.1

What are some different experiences that you might provide to students to help them see why $5x + 2$ is not the same as $7x$ or 7?

Teachers might handle students' inappropriate combining of terms to force closure in at least three different ways:

- By identifying like terms and focusing on combining terms that are alike
- By emphasizing order of operations (e.g., if you have $5x + 2$, you must multiply before you can add, so you cannot go any further because you do not know what you are multiplying 5 by)
- By substituting values into each expression (in this case, $5x + 2$ and $7x$) to show that they do not result in the same value, so they are not equivalent (Tirosh, Even, and Robinson 1998)

An additional way to help students make sense of this issue is to draw on an experientially real context. Such a context may be an authentic life situation, a situation involving a mathematical problem, or a problem in pure mathematics. In each case, the context should be "real for the students and should serve as a basis on which a mathematical concept can be built" (Tabach and Friedlander 2008, p. 223). For example, algebra tiles, which provide an area representation for the algebraic terms (refer back to fig. 2.4), can help students focus on x^2 as represented by the area of a square with dimensions x by x, whereas x is represented by the length of a rectangle with dimensions 1 by x. For a rich and detailed example of how contexts can be used to support students' understanding of the rules of symbolic manipulation (and thus avoid an inappropriate rush to closure), see Tabach and Friedlander (2008).

In students' early experiences with writing expressions, they face a major shift in symbolizing. Previously, when they wrote a two-character expression—say, 34—each character represented a place value, Yet, when they encounter a two-character expression such as $3x$, they discover that the x is not a digit in the ones place. Rather, an implicit multiplication takes place between the x and the 3. Textbooks tend to make this shift in symbolizing quickly, often without making the indicated multiplication explicit. Teachers can continue to use $3 \times x$ or $3 \cdot x$ over a period of time to connect these implicit meanings. As students become more familiar with this meaning, they can be asked, "What does '$3x$' *mean*?" As you observe all students becoming aware of the implicit multiplication in this symbolization, you can revisit the meaning as needed. Reflect 3.2 provides an opportunity to consider the nature of the shift in symbolizing that students in your classroom experience.

Reflect 3.2

Carefully look at the way in which your textbook makes the transition from using a multiplication symbol to implicit multiplication. Does it provide any support for students making the transition? If not, consider asking your students questions like, "What does '$3x$' *mean*?" Use these kinds of questions to see how well students can articulate the meaning of the expressions that you are studying. Reflect on your observations and discuss them with your colleagues.

Variables

Even after three years of algebra instruction, some students still do not understand what letters represent in algebra (Stacey and MacGregor 1997). They have seen letters used in many different ways, such as *p* standing for *page* in "p. 4" or *cm* standing for *centimeter* (or *centimeters*) in the standard metric abbreviation. When students hear teachers say something like, "*C* is cost," they might think that *C* stands for the word *cost* rather than for a *value*. Pointing out this algebraic meaning of a letter used as a variable can be helpful to students. Sometimes, too, a statement such as "*n* stands for nickels" supports students' erroneous perception that a letter stands for a word rather than a value; after all, *nickel* begins with the letter *n*. A strategy to address this issue is to choose as variables letters that are different from those that begin easily associated words.

Letters in algebra can also be confusing because students have previously worked with letters in other contexts, and in some of those, letters have represented numbers (for instance, π). Furthermore, students find that when letters show up in algebra, they are used like numbers in the sense that they appear in expressions and equations with operation symbols, just as numbers do. The most significant difference between letters and numerals, however, is that "numerals represent a single number but letters can represent, simultaneously yet individually, many different numbers" (Wagner 1983). Consider, for example, x in $x < 15$.

Another common source of confusion among students is the misperception that different letters must represent different values. For example, given the equations $5x - 15 = 20$ and $5y - 15 = 20$, students sometimes think that x and y should have different values because they are different letters. Reflect 3.3 offers an opportunity to consider whether you have observed confusion of this sort in students in your classroom.

See Reflect 3.3 on p. 104.

← ← ← stop reflect

If your students think that different variables must have different values, you might illustrate that this is not the case by

Reflect 3.3

Have students in your classroom struggled with the idea that different letters can represent the same value? If so, what are some strategies that you have used to help students work through their confusion?

writing the same equation multiple times but with a different letter representing the variable each time (e.g., $3x = 15$, $3y = 15$, $3a = 15$) and having the students solve the equation for all the differently named variables. You can then use this set of examples to generate a discussion with students about different variables representing the same value.

Representations

In our discussion of Essential Understanding 4*b*, we emphasized that algebraic ideas can be represented and analyzed in multiple ways—in words, contexts, graphs, tables, and symbols. Reflect 3.4 asks you to consider multiple representations of the idea of slope, as an illustration of this idea.

Reflect 3.4

What are the different ways in which *slope* is represented in contexts, tables, graphs, and symbols?

➔ **Essential Understanding 4*b***
Functions can be represented in multiple ways—in algebraic symbols, situations, graphs, verbal descriptions, tables, and so on—and these representations, and the links among them, are useful in analyzing patterns of change.

For students to understand what the slope of a line is, they should be able to talk about it as a rate of change, express it as a rate in real life (e.g., dollars per shirt, miles per hour), identify it as the ratio of the change in y to the change in x in a graph, think of it as the additive rate of change in the y-column of a table (when x increases by 1), and recognize it as m in an equation of the form $y = mx + b$. Not only do students need to know each of these aspects of the concept of slope, but they also should be able to coordinate these meanings in relationship with one another. For instance, students should be able to coordinate the ratio of rise to run with the changes in the y- and x- columns of a table, as well as the vertical and horizontal change in a graph. Which representations of slope are predominant in mathematics instruction? This is the question on which Reflect 3.5 focuses.

Reflect 3.5

Reflect on the experiences and tasks related to slope that you offer your students. What representations receive the most attention? Which receive the least? Why?

Each individual representation offers a snapshot of a mathematical idea. In addition, each has its strengths and limitations (Essential Understanding 4*d*). For example, although a table of values gives many individual instances of a relationship between two variables and provides a natural bridge from studies of patterns in elementary school, it does not provide a holistic view of how the relationship acts over a period of time. Not only is it important to encourage students to use particular representations at different times and in different situations, but it is also important to allow them to choose for themselves which representation to use and to have them identify the strengths and limitations of the various representations. Although each representation has its drawbacks, their collective use can aid in avoiding the disadvantages of individual representations and can help students build understanding of important algebraic ideas (Kaput 1992). Connections among representations are the focus of Reflect 3.6.

Essential Understanding 4*d*
Some representations of a function may be more useful than others, depending on how they are used.

Reflect 3.6

In what ways do you prompt students to translate among representations when you teach? Does your textbook provide opportunities to support this work? If not, how else might you incorporate multi-representational tasks into your instruction?

Grounding early algebraic experiences in familiar contexts can help students to see the relevance of algebra to everyday life. In fact, connecting mathematical ideas to everyday contexts in this way can be especially important for students for whom English is not their first language (Gibbons 2009). It is often helpful to students to use different representations together and to discuss the strengths and limitations of each one. For example, whereas a table provides specific points that are on the line or curve, a graph allows students to see the nature of a line or curve over a broad set of points and can help them understand, for instance, why we classify functions according to their membership in different "families" (Essential Understanding 4*c*).

Essential Understanding 4c
One important way of describing functions is by identifying the rate at which the variables change together. It is useful to group functions into families *with similar patterns of change because these functions, and the situations that they model, share certain general characteristics.*

Current technology, including the graphing calculator, has made the processes of exploring different relationships and making connections among various representations increasingly efficient. Yet, teachers must take care in allowing their students to use technology to explore and solve problems. Reflect 3.7 encourages you to think about the role of technology in your algebra instruction.

← ← ←

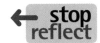

stop reflect
See Reflect 3.7 on p. 106.

It is important to have students examine functions in multiple windows on the calculator for a number of reasons. Sufficiently small window settings can make a curve (for example, a graph of a

Reflect 3.7

In what ways do you use graphing calculators and other technology in your classroom? What positive effects of using technology have you experienced in your instruction? What issues or sources of confusion have you sometimes seen when your students use technology to explore linear and nonlinear relationships?

quadratic relationship) appear to be linear, for instance. Or students may scale the axes of their graphs in such a way that they misrepresent the actual function that the students have graphed. Even the way in which the pixels are set can contribute to a misleading graph. For example, if students zoom in on a graph, they may think that it is built from "steps" instead of being smooth, because the pixels give the graph this appearance. Exploring a range of values is also important when students look at the table on the calculator. Because the window of the graphing calculator allows students to look only at some values, having students scroll up and down on the table to get a sense of other values is important to ensuring that they do not think that a function "quits" after the values shown on the screen.

Students have been found to have difficulties in reading graphs qualitatively (Dugdale 1993). Interpreting graphs in a global, or holistic, way is essential to students' understanding of functions. It is especially easy to confuse a graph of the height of an object over time with *the path of the object.* As we explored in our discussion of Reflect 2.3, in the graph of the relationship between distance and height when someone kicks a soccer ball, the horizontal axis does *not* show the horizontal location of the ball on the soccer field, as many students might think. Rather, the x-axis shows elapsed time. When a projectile is launched straight upward, its path of motion has no horizontal motion at all! Thinking about graphs holistically, both in creating them and in interpreting them, is important, although challenging. Reflect 3.8 illustrates the challenge involved in analyzing and representing relationships between variables holistically.

Reflect 3.8

Create a graph for each of the following scenarios. What are the crucial characteristics to think about holistically in the creation of these graphs?

a. A woman takes a ride on a Ferris wheel.

b. A man sprints to the far end of the gym, stops and rests, and then sprints back.

Graphs can be analyzed and explored holistically by using Computer-Based Ranger 2 (CBR 2), a data-collection device that connects to graphing calculators, available from Texas Instruments. For example, one application allows students to try to "walk the graph." In this application, students are given a graph of a distance-time relationship, and they have to consider where to stand to match the y-intercept and what distance to move from the starting point for each second of time that passes. Although students know what the dependent and independent variables are, this kind of physical engagement can help them develop a better understanding of the relationship between what is happening in a situation and how the situation appears in the graphical representation.

Friedlander and Tabach (2001) suggest a set of activities for engaging students in working with multiple representations in algebra. They suggest that teachers first ask questions that require students to analyze each component of a problem's original presentation and make some extrapolations or draw conclusions. Even when a problem does not require it, they encourage teachers to make explicit requests for translations among representations. Finally, they suggest that it is important to ask students complex and open-ended questions. For example, students might be asked to choose their own method of representation and solution path or to pose reflective questions. The reflective questions might require students to describe the work that they have done and explain why it makes sense, comment on another student's work or strategy (either of which the teacher could provide), write a question, or reflect on particular mathematical ideas (for example, discussing advantages and disadvantages of particular representations).

Writing and Solving Equations

Although students come from elementary school classrooms in which they have solved for unknowns in problems like $3 + \square = 16$, the shift to using a letter to represent an unknown can be confusing. Moreover, when students first start using letters to write equations, it is important to ask them to describe the relationships that they are representing in words and to reason about the expressions involved. A classic case of confusion about the use of letters to represent unknowns involved 150 entering MIT students who were asked to write an equation, using as variables S and P, to represent the statement, "At this university there are six times as many students as professors." This relationship can be represented by the equation $6P = S$. The most common error was to reverse the relationship by writing $6S = P$, a literal translation of the statement (Rosnick 1981). Reflect 3.9 probes how you would respond to your students if they made this error.

Reflect 3.9

Suppose that your students were writing an equation to express the relationship between students (S) and professors (P) in the statement, "At this university there are six times as many students as professors," and that they produced a literal translation of the statement by writing $6S = P$.

What questions might you ask them to scaffold their understanding of the faulty reasoning behind their incorrect equation?

Asking scaffolding questions can help students to reason through a problem (Lochhead and Mestre 1988). For example, if as Reflect 3.9 asks you to suppose, your students produced the incorrect equation $6S = P$, you might ask a sequence of questions:

- "What does S stand for? What does P stand for?"
- "Are there more students or professors on campus?"
- "What if the university had just one professor? How many students would there be?"
- "What if the university had 10 professors? How many students would there be?"
- "What if there were 15 professors?"

The questions that we ask students can help them to make sense of and reason through the process of writing equations.

Students also need ample opportunities to work on translating words and contexts into symbols. One way to handle and ultimately eliminate common mistakes is to select problems that are designed to elicit the mistakes. For example, Narode and Lochhead (1985) suggest asking students to use the letters F and Y to develop an equation that can be used calculate the number of feet in a given number of yards. This problem prompts students to express the mathematical relationship between feet and yards by writing an equation in which they very well may make the same mistake that the entering MIT students made. If they write the erroneous equation $3F = Y$, they will be giving a literal translation of the statement, "There are three feet in a yard." They may indeed set up the problem incorrectly and talk about F and Y as being feet and yards. However, by eliciting the anticipated errors, teachers can carefully engage students in talking about them and recognizing why and how their thinking is problematic.

Verbal descriptions typically accompany much of the mathematics that we do, and these descriptions in words can influence how students learn to make sense of equations. As an example, consider Reflect 3.10.

Reflect 3.10

How would you read the following equation aloud?

$$-2x + 8 = 16$$

Does the way in which you read an equation aloud convey the *meaning* of the equation? The equation $-2x + 8 = 16$ is often read as, "Negative two x plus eight is sixteen," but it can also be read as, "Negative two times some number plus eight equals sixteen," or even as, "What number can I multiply by negative two, then add eight, and get sixteen?" Furthermore, as we work through the process of solving this equation, we typically explain the steps to solve by using verbal descriptions. Reflect 3.11 invites you to think about your own verbalizations.

Reflect 3.11

How would you verbalize the solution to $-2x + 8 = 16$?

If you say, "What might I do solve this equation?" what mathematics are you highlighting?

What if you ask, "What do I do to *both sides* of this equation to solve it?"

What if you covered up the $2x$ and asked, "What can I add to eight to get sixteen?" and then asked, "So, what times negative two gives me eight?"

The first two of these verbalizations highlight the "undoing" of the operations. The first ("What might I do to solve this equation?") is more open-ended, whereas the second emphasizes the fact that when we are solving an equation, the equals sign requires us to perform the same operation on both sides to ensure equivalence. To draw further attention to the importance of this point, a natural follow-up question might be, "Why do I have to subtract eight from both sides?"

The third verbalization, however, highlights the operations that are being done in the equation, or "forward thinking." In other words, it emphasizes the structure of the equation and what the equation means. Kieran and Chalouh (1993) argue that when we engage students *only* in "undoing" operations (like the first verbalization described), teaching "can sometimes be counterproductive to students' developing an understanding of (*a*) an equation as a balanced entity and (*b*) the solving procedure of performing the same operation on both sides of the equation" (p. 61).

If we focus on verbalizing the solution through the undoing of the operations, we have different ways of expressing the solution. Two examples follow:

- "In solving this problem, I would subtract eight from both sides first. That leaves negative two x equals eight. I would then divide both sides by negative two and get negative four."
- "When I solve this problem, I can start by subtracting eight from both sides because I want to get the negative two x by itself to solve for x. When I subtract eight from both sides, I get negative two x plus eight minus eight equals sixteen minus eight. Since I am subtracting the same thing from both sides, the two sides stay equal because..."

Big Idea 5

General algorithms exist for solving many kinds of equations; these algorithms are broadly applicable for solving a wide range of similar equations. However, for some problems or situations, alternatives to these general algorithms may be more elegant, efficient, or informative.

Essential Understanding 5*b*
Linear equations can be solved by symbolic, graphical, and numerical methods. On some occasions and in some contexts, one solution method may be more elegant, efficient, or informative than another.

It is important to recognize that no verbal description truly captures everything in the mathematical representation that is under consideration. For example, when we say "two x," we are not explicitly recognizing the implied multiplication. Because verbal descriptions tend to accompany almost everything we do in algebra, we should consider them carefully. In fact, there is strong evidence that when teachers do not make explicit for themselves the characteristics of verbal and written descriptions that they consider to be effective, they have only a tacit understanding when they look for evidence in assessing student work (Morgan 1998).

Another challenge of teaching equation solving is freeing students from the belief that there is only one correct way to solve particular sorts of equations (for example, the algorithm for solving linear equations, which we explored in our discussion of Big Idea 5). By developing facility with only one solution process, students gain very limited knowledge of the mathematical principles that support the steps of the algorithm. For example, students may come to believe that dividing both expressions in an equation by a constant is allowed only in the final step (that is, when the equation is of the form $ax = b$). Rather, there are many ways to solve equations, an idea captured in Essential Understanding 5*b*. As Star and Rittle-Johnson (2008; see also Rittle-Johnson and Star [2007]) have reported, when students are exposed to and expected to learn multiple methods for solving equations, they can become flexible in the use of multiple methods and gain conceptual knowledge about important principles related to equation solving, such as equivalence and the axioms of equality.

Conclusion

This chapter has highlighted some issues that commonly arise in the teaching of expressions, equations, and functions. Some of these stem from students' previous experiences—for example, their work with the equals sign or in writing numbers. Others relate to students' understanding of the multiple representations for expressing the mathematical ideas with which the students are grappling. Through careful planning and consideration, you can be prepared to discuss these issues and can turn them into learning opportunities for your students. We have suggested some options, and we hope that you continue to explore these issues, along with the big ideas of expressions, equations, and functions, with your colleagues.

References

Blanton, Maria, Linda Levi, Terry Wayne Crites, and Barbara J. Dougherty. *Developing Essential Understanding of Algebraic Thinking for Teaching Mathematics in Grades 3–5*. Essential Understanding Series. Reston, Va.: National Council of Teachers of Mathematics, 2011.

Brown, Susan A., R. James Breulin, Mary H. Wiltjer, Katherine M. Degner, Susan K. Eddins, Michael T. Edwards, Neva A. Metcalf, Natalie Jakucyn, and Zalman Usiskin. *Algebra*. University of Chicago School Mathematics Project. Chicago: Wright Group/McGraw-Hill, 2008.

Chazan, Daniel. *Beyond Formulas in Mathematics and Teaching: Dynamics of the High School Algebra Classroom*. New York: Teachers College Press, 2000.

Chazan, Daniel, and Michal Yerushalmy. "On Appreciating the Cognitive Complexity of School Algebra: Research on Algebra Learning and Directions of Curricular Change." In *A Research Companion to "Principles and Standards for School Mathematics,"* edited by Jeremy Kilpatrick, W. Gary Martin, and Deborah Schifter, pp. 123–35. Reston, Va.: National Council of Teachers of Mathematics, 2003.

Common Core State Standards Initiative (CCSSI). *Common Core State Standards for Mathematics. Common Core State Standards (College- and Career-Readiness Standards and K–12 Standards in English Language Arts and Math)*. Washington, D.C.: National Governors Association Center for Best Practices and the Council of Chief State School Officers, 2010. http://www.corestandards.org.

Cooney, Thomas J., Sybilla Beckmann, and Gwendolyn M. Lloyd. *Developing Essential Understanding of Functions for Teaching Mathematics in Grades 9–12*. Essential Understanding Series. Reston, Va.: National Council of Teachers of Mathematics, 2010.

Dugdale, Sharon. "Functions and Graphs—Perspectives on Student Thinking." In *Integrating Research on the Graphical Representation of Functions*, edited by Thomas Romberg, Elizabeth Fennema, and Thomas Carpenter, pp. 101–30. Hillsdale, N.J.: Lawrence Erlbaum Associates, 1993.

Education Development Center (EDC). *Algebra 1*. CME Project. Boston: Pearson, 2009.

Fey, James T., M. Kathleen Heid, Richard Good, Charlene Sheets, Glendon Blume, and Rose Mary Zbiek. *Computer-Intensive Algebra: A Technological Approach*. Dedham, Mass.: Janson Publications, 1995.

Friedlander, Alex, and Michal Tabach. "Promoting Multiple Representations in Algebra." In *The Roles of Representation in School Mathematics*, 2001 Yearbook of the National Council of Teachers of Mathematics (NCTM), edited by Albert A. Cuoco, pp. 173–85. Reston, Va.: NCTM, 2001.

Gibbons, Pauline. *English Learners, Academic Literacy, and Thinking: Learning in the Challenge Zone*. Portsmouth, N.H.: Heinemann, 2009.

Heid, M. Kathleen. "A Technology-Intensive Functional Approach to the Emergence of Algebraic Thinking." In *Approaches to Algebra: Perspectives for Research and Teaching*, edited by Nadine Bednarz, Carolyn Kieran, and Lesley Lee, pp. 239–55. Dordrecht, The Netherlands: Kluwer, 1996.

Kaput, James. "Technology and Mathematics Education." In *Handbook of Research on Mathematics Teaching and Learning*, edited by Douglas A. Grouws, pp. 515–56. New York: Macmillan, 1992.

Kieran, Carolyn, and Louise Chalouh. "Prealgebra: The Transition from Arithmetic to Algebra." In *Research Ideas for the Classroom: Middle Grades Mathematics*, edited by Douglas Owens, pp. 179–98. Reston, Va.: National Council of Teachers of Mathematics, 1993.

Knuth, Eric J., Ana C. Stephens, Nicole M. McNeil, and Martha W. Alibali. "Does Understanding the Equal Sign Matter? Evidence from Solving Equations." *Journal for Research in Mathematics Education* 37 (July 2006): 297–312.

Lappan, Glenda, James T. Fey, William M. Fitzgerald, Susan N. Friel, and Elizabeth D. Phillips. *Frogs, Fleas, and Painted Cubes*. Connected Mathematics. Needham, Mass., and Upper Saddle River, N.J.: Pearson Prentice Hall, 2004a.

———. *Variables and Patterns: Introducing Algebra*. Connected Mathematics. Needham, Mass., and Upper Saddle River, N.J.: Pearson Prentice Hall, 2004b.

Lochhead, Jack, and José P. Mestre. "From Words to Algebra: Mending Misconceptions." In *The Ideas of Algebra, K–12*, 1988 Yearbook of the National Council of Teachers of Mathematics (NCTM), edited by Arthur F. Coxford, pp. 127–35. Reston, Va.: NCTM, 1988.

Malloy, Carol, Jack Price, Teri Willard, and Leon L. Sloan. *Pre-Algebra*. Glencoe Mathematics. Columbus, Ohio: Glencoe/McGraw-Hill, 2005.

Morgan, Candia. *Writing Mathematically: The Discourse of Investigation*. London: Falmer, 1998.

Narode, Ronald, and Jack Lochhead. "What Do You Think?" *Impact on Instructional Improvement* 19 (Spring 1985): 56–62.

National Council of Teachers of Mathematics (NCTM). *Curriculum and Evaluation Standards for School Mathematics*. Reston, Va.: NCTM, 1989.

——. *Principles and Standards for School Mathematics*. Reston, Va.: NCTM, 2000.

——. *Curriculum Focal Points for Prekindergarten through Grade 8 Mathematics: A Quest for Coherence*. Reston, Va.: NCTM, 2006.

——. *Focus in High School Mathematics: Reasoning and Sense Making*. Reston, Va.: NCTM, 2009.

Otto, Albert Dean, Janet H. Caldwell, Cheryl Ann Lubinski, and Sarah Wallus Hancock. *Developing Essential Understanding of Multiplication and Division for Teaching Mathematics in Grades 3–5*. Essential Understanding Series. Reston, Va.: National Council of Teachers of Mathematics, 2011.

Phelps, Steve, and Michael Todd Edwards. "New Life for an Old Topic: Completing the Square Using Technology." *Mathematics Teacher* 104 (April 2010): 230–36.

Rittle-Johnson, Bethany, and Jon R. Star. "Does Comparing Solution Methods Facilitate Conceptual and Procedural Knowledge? An Experimental Study on Learning to Solve Equations." *Journal of Educational Psychology* 99 (August 2007): 561–74.

Roodhardt, A., J. Burrill, M. S. Spence, and P. Christiansen. "Growth." In *Mathematics in Context*, edited by National Center for Research in Mathematical Sciences Education and Freudenthal Institute. Chicago: Encyclopædia Britannica, 1998.

Rosnick, Peter. "Some Misconceptions concerning the Concept of Variable." *Mathematics Teacher* 74 (September 1981): 418–20.

Schoenfeld, Alan, and Abraham Arcavi. "On the Meaning of Variable." *Mathematics Teacher* 81 (September 1988): 420–27.

Schwartz, Judah, and Michal Yerushalmy. "Getting Students to Function in and with Algebra." In *The Concept of Function: Aspects of Epistemology and Pedagogy*, MAA Notes, vol. 25, edited by Ed Dubinsky and Guershon Harel, pp. 261–89. Washington, D.C.: Mathematical Association of America, 1992.

Sinclair, Nathalie, David Pimm, and Melanie Skelin. *Developing Essential Understanding of Geometry for Teaching Mathematics in Grades 6–8*. Essential Understanding Series. Reston, Va.: National Council of Teachers of Mathematics, forthcoming.

Stacey, Kaye, and Mollie MacGregor. "Ideas about Symbolism That Students Bring to Algebra." *Mathematics Teacher* 90 (February 1997): 110–13.

Star, Jon R., and Bethany Rittle-Johnson. "Flexibility in Problem Solving: The Case of Equation Solving." *Learning and Instruction* 18 (December 2008): 565–79.

——. “Making Algebra Work: Instructional Strategies That Deepen Student Understanding, within and between Representations.” *ERS Spectrum* 27 (September 2009): 11–18.

Tabach, Michal, and Alex Friedlander. “The Role of Context in Learning Beginning Algebra.” *Algebra and Algebraic Thinking in School Mathematics*, Seventieth Yearbook of the National Council of Teachers of Mathematics (NCTM), edited by Carole E. Greenes, pp. 223–32. Reston, Va.: NCTM, 2008.

Tirosh, Dina, Ruhama Even, and Naomi Robinson. “Simplifying Algebraic Expressions: Teacher Awareness and Teaching Approaches.” *Educational Studies in Mathematics* 35 (January 1998): 51–64.

Usiskin, Zalman. “Conceptions of School Algebra and Uses of Variables.” *The Ideas of Algebra, K–12*, 1988 Yearbook of the National Council of Teachers of Mathematics (NCTM), edited by Arthur F. Coxford, pp. 8–19. Reston, Va.: National Council of Teachers of Mathematics, 1988.

Wagner, Sigrid. “What Are These Things Called Variables?” *Mathematics Teacher* 76 (October 1983): 474–79.

Weeks, Audrey. “Connecting Complex Roots to a Parabola’s Graph.” *ON-Math* 1 (Spring 2003). http://www.nctm.org/eresources/view_article.asp?article_id=6168&page=1.

Titles in the Essential Understanding Series

The Essential Understanding Series gives teachers the deep understanding that they need to teach challenging topics in mathematics. Students encounter such topics across the pre-K–grade 12 curriculum, and teachers who understand the big ideas related to each topic can give maximum support as students develop their own understanding and make vital connections.

Number and Numeration for Teaching Mathematics in Prekindergarten–Grade 2
ISBN 978-0-87353-629-5 Stock No. 13492

Addition and Subtraction for Teaching Mathematics in Prekindergarten–Grade 2
ISBN 978-0-87353-664-6 Stock No. 13792

Geometry and Measurement for Teaching Mathematics in Prekindergarten–Grade 2
ISBN 978-0-87353-665-3 Stock No. 13793

Rational Numbers for Teaching Mathematics in Grades 3–5
ISBN 978-0-87353-630-1 Stock No. 13493

Algebraic Thinking for Teaching Mathematics in Grades 3–5
ISBN 978-0-87353-668-4 Stock No. 13796

Multiplication and Division for Teaching Mathematics in Grades 3–5
ISBN 978-0-87353-667-7 Stock No. 13795

Geometry and Measurement for Teaching Mathematics in Grades 3–5
ISBN 978-0-87353-669-1 Stock No. 13797

Ratios, Proportions, and Proportional Reasoning for Teaching Mathematics in Grades 6–8
ISBN 978-0-87353-622-6 Stock No. 13482

Expressions, Equations, and Functions for Teaching Mathematics in Grades 6–8
ISBN 978-0-87353-670-7 Stock No. 13798

Geometry for Teaching Mathematics in Grades 6–8
ISBN 978-0-87353-691-2 Stock No. 14122

Statistics for Teaching Mathematics in Grades 6–8
ISBN 978-0-87353-672-1 Stock No. 13800

Functions for Teaching Mathematics in Grades 9–12
ISBN 978-0-87353-623-3 Stock No. 13483

Geometry for Teaching Mathematics in Grades 9–12
ISBN 978-0-87353-692-9 Stock No. 14123

Proof and Proving for Teaching Mathematics in Grades 9–12
ISBN 978-0-87353-675-2 Stock No. 13803

Statistics for Teaching Mathematics in Grades 9–12
ISBN 978-0-87353-676-9 Stock No. 13804

Mathematical Reasoning for Teaching Mathematics in Prekindergarten–Grade 8
ISBN 978-0-87353-666-0 Stock No. 13794

Visit www.nctm.org/catalog for details and ordering information.